Love That Lasts

Poetry & Prose
By Humera Mohammed

About the Book

Love That Lasts is a collection of poetry and prose defining love and expressing love. We make connections in life to explore the bounty and beauty of relation by blood, relation by heart and soul to experience the pleasure of love until we come best out of love and worst out of love.

The biggest tragedy of life is to testify to what we love in terms of valuing and accepting what is coming in our way. The collection has answers to prolonged questions questioning love and justifications over lack of acknowledgement of love in the form of prose. The book Love that lasts highlights the importance of understanding the state of life. It's about discovering every human emotion and life respectively.

Love That Lasts is a poetic journey through the depths of love, its strength, and its ability to endure. In a world where love is often seen as fleeting, this collection serves as a reminder that true love never fades; it transforms, grows, and finds new ways to stay.

Through heartfelt verses, Humera Mohammed captures the essence of love in all its forms—the quiet devotion of companionship, the ache of longing, the resilience of a heart that refuses to forget, and the warmth of a love that withstands time. Each poem is a reflection of emotions we all carry, a gentle reminder that love is not measured by moments but by the way it lingers in our souls.

Whether you have loved and lost, found love in unexpected places, or still believe in love's unwavering presence, Love That Lasts is for you. Let these words wrap around your heart and remind you that love, once given, is never truly lost—it lives on, always.

"Love That Lasts" is more than just a collection of poems; it is a promise—of love that stays, of feelings that never fade, and of the unspoken words that live forever in the heart.

About the Author

Humera Mohammed is an Amazon bestselling author from Hyderabad with her debut book It's You I Ink. She is a poetess, content writer, and creative writer, currently pursuing her undergraduate degree.

For Humera, writing isn't just words—it's how she shares life and emotions. She believes the world needs listeners, people who walk beside you without expectations. She dreams of being like the moon, a silent companion in people's darkest moments. Through her poetry, she hopes to be that voice, that presence, that guiding light. She believes that love, like poetry, is meant to be felt, cherished, and remembered. With a heart full of kindness and empathy, she writes to capture the essence of love that endures—beyond time, beyond words, beyond the fleeting nature of life itself.

Acknowledgment

With a heart full of gratitude, I extend my deepest appreciation to everyone who has been a part of my journey in bringing Love That Lasts to life.

To the ones who have loved me, supported me, and believed in my words, you are the reason this book exists. Your kindness, encouragement, and unwavering faith in me have been my greatest strength.
To my family, whose love is the foundation of all that I am—thank you for being my anchor and my inspiration. Your support means more than words can express.

To my readers, those who find pieces of themselves in my poetry, who embrace the emotions woven into these pages, you are the heartbeat of this book. Your love for words, for feelings, and for stories that endure is what makes this journey worthwhile.

And finally,_ to love itself—the most powerful, transformative force in the world. May it continue to inspire, heal, and remind us of all that love, when true, always lasts.

Love & prayers
Humera Mohammed

Contents

Poetry

It was love,
It happened —
Now, no other game remains ahead.
One glance was enough
To make you mine,
That very glance
Is enough to spend a lifetime.

I've loved everything from far
But I want to love you from close.
I've waited for this moment to come
But I'm letting you go this time.
For things that come late—
I heard it's worth the wait.

I feel more of pain
And less of love.
As maybe least of you—
As I found you
At the peak of pain.
Now I feel more of you
And least of love.

How do I tell you? My love —
I don't want anything from you,
Rather, I have so much to offer you.

I cannot see the pain in your eyes
For all that you hide inside —
Sleepless nights, restless heart,
For all that you go through alone.

My heart aches—
It aches for you.

Was it too easy for you?
To act like nothing happened?

I want to make you laugh hard,
Smile even more.
I want to make your eyes shine
Like never before.

For how long should I keep ranting? Oh love —
I want to give you hope, dreams,
I want to give you
The love of the whole world.

How do I tell you? My beloved —
If I were to rip out your complete self
And owe my all happiness, goodness of fate...

If I were to introduce you to life
And make it happen — colour you joy —

Then, infinite times,
I would choose to exchange
All of your worst things as mine,
And give you back
All of my best things as yours.

I always tell you,
But you never listen.

You're my only love —
And for you,
I can move mountains.

Yet, by your call,
I can even disappear
From every elsewhere.

Love is love,
Love is a beautiful desire —
Of being loved,
And sometimes being touched by the beloved —

But lust is not love.
Lust is when it's wrapped beautifully with lies,
To set the cage
For the human bird to be trapped.

And to leave them traumatized for a lifetime,
For not believing in people —
And in love itself.

The human-form beast
With an innocent love mask —
It hunts the body,
While the marks never fade —
Even after watering it a thousand times.

Oh, the chick inside the very eggshell —
Beware of the world that's beautifully ugly.
Then it makes you dream and glorifies you
To dupe you in the name of love.

Because
Love is when it's true —
It covers up your body and flaws.

And when
Lust is when it's deception —
It undresses and takes advantage of you.

People don't lose virginity
But they lose —
Believing in people
Who truly want to love them,
And falling in love all over again
By the fear of past outsources.

And I found love —
Even in pain, ignorance, and left behind.
And after you,
I will still burn out love, longing, and waiting.

For this is love —
Pure and eternal.
It only falls once,
And loves the only one, an infinite time.

And in love —
I find a strange self-surrendered completely,
Who is courageous, powerful, and stubborn.

I wore your shirt and fragrance today,
But yet I couldn't feel you.

I cried at my worst today,
But yet weeping hasn't solaced me.
My heart aches in your absence—
Is there any way of your comeback?

You were all mine,
And I was all yours.

But yet I feel detached and departed.

I'm not happy,
Neither do I have the energy to pretend.
Why doesn't God take me to you?
I no longer feel like living anymore.

Never surrender yourself
To the flow of life

Never give the rope
To the one who can pull you down

Your eyes are full of hopes,
Your smile is full of happiness.

Ask me what's the most beautiful thing
In the whole world—
I'll chant you, just you.

You're the most kindest,
You're the most gentle.

Ask me who would've owned my heart
In the whole world—
I'll chant you, just you.

Peace. Healer. Love.
Darling, you tell me—
What you're not amongst these?

But how come I not tell you,
Magic within you
Is what inspires me the most.

There is always a good person
In every bad person you meet.

There is always a bad person
In every good person you meet.

And there is always a character
You never met
In the person you meet.

Sometimes—
Or maybe most of the time—
We stop loving ourselves,

Despite unloving our beloved ones,
Who fragile
The most beautiful part within us.

People can fake tears.
People can lie honestly.
People can pretend to change.

They've no limit or restrictions—
They've free will
To break hearts
And burn homes.

Sometimes people
Around you break something in you
That can never be fixed
And healed.

The heart feels so heavy inside—
As if it's occupied.

The emptiness echoes within me,
As if there is a volcano of emotion
Coming out of it
Despite settling down.

I fear if it takes my life...
I wonder if I take my own life.

I'm not afraid of battles—
But anxiety, depression, and
Disorder make me pathetic.

Before I could face off with people,
I'm not able to make
Eye contact with myself either.

Don't you portray me
As an over-thinker, darling.

How effortless is it
To make an effort
To create an image
Just to get sympathy?
How pity.

Was that all you knew of me—
From years, from close?

I'm not sorry for all the things that happened,
But I feel I deserved a good storyline—
Or maybe a fine listener
Who had my back,

Listening to the unspoken words
I kept inside.

The eyes haven't cried for too long,
As if they're completely drained.

I wanted to run to my beloved ones,
But they seemed more disturbed than I am.

But there were these few people
Who loved me to the moon and its back.

I still lacked the courage to speak,
To open my heart and scars to show.

I knew deep down
There's something missing.
I also knew if I exist—
More of my parts do exist.

I took tiny steps toward life,
Assembling, to put in order
The scattered pieces of my heart—
To heal and live,
Making myself as proud as I can be.

And when my soul
Will be taken out of my body,
And when life splashes backwards—

I want to be recalled
With all the big achievements,
Goals I had in my palm.

I want to be remembered
As the inspirational beam—
Enlightening the world,
and making people believe in
Empathy, love, and magic.

I want to be as kind
As wild as I can be.

I want to be bright as the sun,
And calming as the moon can be.

A metaphor that brings chaos—
And nostalgia back.

Creating lasting memories
That can't be recreated again.

I want a legacy
That'll be remembered for life.

I'll be myself, If I get to get
What I prayed for—
In order to live.

How do I tell you
What's in my messy head?

I've gotten mixed feelings...
Even I don't know when
My mood shifts—
From joy,
To sadism,
To anxiousness,
Probably to happiness.

I change in fractions of seconds.
I can turn my life up and down,

But still show tenacity and mettle—
To live,
And to be happy.

What more can I give to the world?
A part of my heart...
Or a piece of poetry writing.

Love isn't erroneous,

But the course of action taken—
In love,
For love—

Can portray everything in love
As wrong
And unacceptable.

What's the point of having a heart
Without experiencing hurt?

What's the point of living life
Without experiencing loss?

Love happens all of the sudden—
It does not seek validation.

In the beautiful valley of life,
Love becomes the place to reside.

For all it takes is the first glimpse
Of a paired eye.

Love happens all of the sudden—
A feeling known, but the person unknown.

It doesn't require name, caste,
Or a following destination—
For what matters is being in love
And being loved back.

Navigating through the shores of life,
Holding hands in the toughest time,
Finding the beauty of seven phases in love—

With someone who promises
To walk through every edge of life.

Confining to share
All the bits of darkness,
In a life that gives closures,
But love—
Love makes you known, heard, and seen.

It accepts flaws,
Values existence,
Despite all the agitation.

You're the art, the dream, the poem.
You're the hope, the love, the magic.

You're the moon, the peace, the home—
All the things I could ever think.

You brought all the things I never asked.
You're the timeless treasure of life.

You're the giver who doesn't count.
You're the angel in the face of a human being.

Before my thoughts could contemplate,
You solved all the problems before I could speak.

You're the prayer that becomes true.
You're the miracle that people believe exists.

In the middle of chaos between *want* and *need*,
You're the One—
The master of all,
The only one I ever wished.

All this is love—
I know.

All I need is you—
I know.

I've crossed
All the seven stages of love—
In love with you.

And this is all I know...

All this is love,
I know.

What is love?
It's when you find home in a person.

What does it look like?
It reflects you like the mirror.

When can I expect it?
It happens all of a sudden.

What does it have to offer?
Peace that you lack often.

How can I find it?
Love itself comes to you.

What does it feel like to be in love?
You've won at the accomplishment of life.

Why does it end with melancholy?
To realize the state of its value.

What does it bring altogether?
Clarity over confusion,
And faith over fear.

How can I know if it's truly love?
If action speaks more than words,
And the heart wins over the mind.

What if it changes?
Love doesn't change—
But people do.

How would I assure if love can happen only once?
Love can happen all over again.
It seeks love, not validation.

I loved you—
Dearly, madly, deeply.

I loved you—
Without knowing you.

I loved you—
Without loving you.

Selflessly.
Hopelessly.
Immensely.

The love burns deep within—
To light the one it deeply loves.

There are still people—
People of love, people in love—
Who can fight with the world
To win over love.

There are still hearts—
Hearts of love, hearts in love—
Who can die for their beloved.

Promises that are sealed,
Promises that are fulfilled.

There are still people—
People with pure hearts,
People with pure love—
Who burn themselves
To make others alive.

And in the state of chaos,
There are still lovers
Who yearn, ache, and compromise.

Because—
Isn't the first principle itself
What it teaches?

That the priority of a lover's happiness
Is to leave… for its own sake.

And after all—
Love is all about happening,
The promise being fulfilled,
The first fight of love
Being worth its first glance.

I've touched you with my eyes
Way before my arms could.

Darling, you always tell me—
There are no such possibilities
Of our destinies colliding together.

But darling,
I feel you more often
Than I could ever feel for myself.

If this isn't beyond love—
To love someone
Without expecting love to reciprocate?

But darling,
I'm here to make every impossible
Possible and happening for you.

I owe my complete self
Way beforehand you would.

Darling, you always tell me—
Love is sick, cruel, and explosive.
But you were the one who introduced it.

How can I detach myself from you?
You live in me,
And I want to live with you.

I'm an old-school love—
With the first sight love theory.

In the middle of the chaos,
I fell harder for you
Way before you would.

I found home in you—
Way before you could.

-First sight

Attraction
Infatuation
Love
Reverence
Worship
Obsession
Death

Forgotten-

All the things,
And every single being
On planet Earth,
Have a mission to accomplish—
To find the pathway of purpose.

With a beautiful life holding equity,
Making dreams, love, and prosperity
Happening.

Coping with heartbreaks,
Separation, and loss.
From highs to lows,
From pretty to worst—
Every single thing taking part
Is necessary.

And all the beings
Going through and through—
To find themselves
In people, places, and things,
With the beautiful gift called life.

Making ways out
And things happening—
From laughs to cries,
Dreams to reality,
Thoughts to decisions,
Happy to melancholy.

And that's a chain of events,
Acknowledging nothing remains usual.

There are stages of life
And phases of age—
Acquiring ourselves
To come out of the nutshell.

For a world that's beautiful and ugly,
And people with love
And miserable masks.

For a life that gives closures,
And time that ripens individuality—

Upbringing dues
Of love and life.

Through and through—
You needed the back.

To all the things,
And every single being—

Becoming a safe place,
A happy persona,
A peace maker.

For not passing
The cartage to the future beings,
As it was imposed aggressively—
Upholding from the past,
Through and through
Decades,
Onto today's beings.

To all the beings—

Becoming the best versions of themselves,
With empathetic nature,
Kind words,
Understanding souls,
Hospitable hearts,
And a beautiful heart
Above all.

I no longer feel like making someone my own,
I no longer feel like maintaining any relationship.

New friends are fine,
But now even calling out to old friends
Doesn't feel right anymore.

Neither do desires,
Nor dreams surround me now.
Nor do I long to bloom again.

When fate is to break,
Scatter,
And wither away—
Then why turn away
From the mirror of the soul?

Now, neither living
Nor giving hope to live feels right.

I don't know why
I no longer feel at home within myself.

Even under the vast, empty sky,
Amidst the wandering stars and moon,

I don't know why
I no longer feel right
Within myself.

Today, once again,
I looked at myself
And felt like crying.

I don't know how many times
I have returned
From my own doorstep.

How can I admire the beautiful sights,
Gaze into mesmerizing, deer-like eyes,
Enjoy the presence of new people
And changing seasons,

When a salty ocean resides
In the shadow of my eyelashes—
It neither stops
Nor hesitates to flow.

Today, once again,
I looked at myself
And felt pity for my own existence.

How did my laughter
Drift away from me?
How did my childhood companion
Grow so distant?

Something has changed
In these passing years—
Something that has altered
Everything once connected to me.

Today, once again,
I looked at myself
And questioned my own presence.

How did the one
Who once lived so freely
Become confined
To one's own thoughts?

The one —
Who once longed
For a vast life,
Now —
Finds no passion left
In living.

Ask my little heart
How it was in love with you—
Immensely, selflessly, hopelessly.

Ask my little heart
How deathful it was to pass every second
In memory of you.

For the times I kept my heart on hold,
For being cold and ruthless with life,
Pretending I'm all okay.

But my love—
You broke, scattered,
And turned my heart into ashes.

It was way too easy to be forgotten,
To be just imaginable.
But you destroyed my pride—
Over the things
I kept on court-rooming myself for,
Over and again,
Since you left.

My heart burned out of love—
Longing, waiting, staying.

Ask my heart how I was in love—
Deeply, completely, madly.

My soul scatters
By every word of your name.

Ask my heart
How far I've lived without you.
It was your fragrance
That kept my house as home.

Ask my little heart—
How I've inked you with my teary eyes.

It's more than I could ever
Describe you through wordings.

How the truth pricks,
How bitter the truth is.

But if I tell the truth—
How true it really is.

Even the best relationships
Waver because of the truth.

But those who hold onto
The thread of relationships with truth—

Believe me,
There is no greater truth
Than truth itself.

Shall we go?
Toward a new journey,
Leaving the destination to the time,
Leaving the past behind.

This time, let's pause for a night
On those unpaved roads.
Let's do what we never even imagined.

Why distract the heart from afar?
Why not hum the tune
That truly resonates within?

Let's walk on an unknown road,
To witness new sights and pleasant weather,
To explore the world's rare, beautiful cities,
To meet new people and gain new experiences.

To find peace of mind,
To embrace the joy of the heart—
Somewhere far away,
In an unfamiliar journey.

Let's go far,
Away from the noise,
Away from constraints,
Away from restrictions,
Away from worries.

Maybe not till the destination,
But at least till where this road ends.

Let's start anew,
Shall we?

I have begun to fear myself now.
My thoughts bring terror,
And my dreams feel suffocating.

There are sins so deep,
That I have started to hate myself.

Darkness feels like home now,
And strangely,
Solitude brings me peace.

I could call out a thousand times,
But the question is—
Will anyone answer now?

To the world,
I am selfish, indifferent, and self-absorbed.
But will anyone ever listen
To my unheard story?

I could still search for hope,
Light,
And happiness—
But is there any joy
Left in living now?

I have left all my matters to time.
Generous, loving—
My Lord is ever-merciful.

But the question is—
Does He still accept me now?

People count my flaws endlessly,
But if I were to hold up a mirror,
How wrong would I appear now?

My eyes shed tears
For no reason these days.

Why this complaint,
This resentment?
What is truly in our hands—
That fate could be altered now?

This silence has begun to pierce me,
As pain, grief, and anger
Push to escape.

If I, too, start wearing a mask
Like everyone else,
Then dignity, sincerity, and grace
Will all be stripped away now.

How important it is
To have someone who understands—

For if every touch only wounds,
Then wouldn't this once-flourishing life
Start to feel like a burden now?

I wonder—
What would the world
Beyond the sky be like?

The One who gives endlessly
Upon a single request—
What would that God be like?

In the movement of these stars,
You pause like the moon.

In this world that walks behind the clouds,
You stay by my side like the moon.

In this vast, empty sky-like world,
You brighten my world like the moon.

Life is a garden—
In every state, it belongs to you.

Sometimes joyful,
Sometimes sorrowful,
Sometimes good,
Sometimes bad,
But in every state, this life is yours.

Bad times feel never-ending,
Yet they always pass.

Sometimes by separating you
From yourself or your loved ones,
Sometimes by testing you
With what is dearest to your heart.

But why do you forget
That no matter how dark the night is,
It's morning always dewy and fresh?

Hard times are merely a test—
The beginning of better days,
Of a brighter tomorrow.

Every steadfast step you take,
Every tear you shed,
In times that shake your heart—
Hold onto it firmly.

In difficult moments,
Make decisions with strength and wisdom.

Hard times are just
The start of good times.

Just never lose to yourself.
Even if the world defeats you
A thousand times—

Never turn away
From your own spirit.

Stay happy.
Stay steadfast.

Because life, in every state, is a garden.

It is through bad times
That we recognize good times.

It is through bad times
That we learn their true worth.

It is through bad times
That we realize
We are stronger than we think.

Endure tough times
Just as eagerly
As you long for the best of days.

Hard times are not so terrible
That you must crave their end.

Time itself is neither good nor bad—
It's how you live that defines it.

So live—
Live as if
This moment is your last.

Live as if
Life itself blossoms through you.

O life, for once,
Be kind to me.

I know you are nothing
But trials and tests—
But just for a moment,
Fill my hands with happiness too.

Yes, I understand—
I am merely a guest in your world,
But grant me at least
One moment of peace,

So that my helplessness
Does not bow before my fate.

Change the course
Of the lines in my palms,
And have mercy
On the tears in my eyes.

I no longer find comfort
In calling someone my own,
I no longer find joy
In maintaining relationships.

New friends are one thing—
But now, even calling out to old friends
Doesn't feel right.

Neither desires
Nor dreams revolve around me anymore,
Nor do I long
Or strive to bloom.

When breaking, shattering,
And being abandoned
Is written in fate—
Then why turn away from regret?

Now, neither living
Nor giving hope to live
Feels right.

I don't know why
I no longer feel at home within myself.

Even beneath the vast, empty sky,
Amidst the circling stars and moon—
I don't know why
I no longer feel right
Within my own being.

In the darkness of the night, I kept covering myself,
With each passing night, I kept forgetting God.

Neither did my eyes open,
Nor did the morning arrive,
Nor did a new day show mercy upon me.

Day by day, my attitude changed,
My state worsened, circumstances shifted,
And somewhere amidst the clouds,
I was lost.

A single spark is enough to start a fire,
But how can a flame ignite on damp wood?

When faith is strong,
A mere drop turns into an ocean.
But when the footsteps waver,
Even the vast sea feels empty.

There was once an era
Where homes were reduced to ashes,
Heads were severed—
Yet not a single forehead
Lifted from prostration.

And I wonder,
In what kind of era do I exist now—
Where it's only about *me*,
As if conscience itself
Has perished.

To embrace someone helpless
And call them your own—
That is love.

To feed the hungry
With your own hands—
That is love.

To stand by someone
In their difficult times—
That is love.

To see someone's tears
Fall from your own eyes—
That is love.

To witness another's sorrows and grief
And consider them your own—
That is love.

To turn mere dust into a home—
That is love.

To cover someone's mistakes
With kindness—
That is love.

To recognize the fragility of glass
And still shape it with care—
That is love.

When someone else's pain
Begins to feel like your own—
That is love.

When someone's presence
becomes a source of peace—
that is love.

When you accept the flaws and mistakes
without being judgmental—
that is love.

When you forgive, over and over,
fearing the very thought of losing—
that is love.

When someone doesn't choose to reciprocate,
but you still choose to love them—
that is beyond love.

When someone doesn't appreciate your efforts,
doesn't acknowledge your existence,
yet again and again,
over and over,
you love them—
that is divine love.

Why regret what has already passed?
Why grieve over what was never written in my fate?

How could I have convinced the one
Who chose to leave?
If staying was an option,
They wouldn't have decided to go.

There is nothing left in life now—
So much of it has already passed,
Let the rest pass too.

These people who resent my change
Without hesitation—
Ask them how silent I remained
When they changed.

Life whispers,
"Give it a chance...
Perhaps a miracle still waits
In the palm of your hand."

I am trying to hold myself together,
Yet somehow, I keep breaking apart.

If there was any meaning in my name,
Then perhaps destiny would have been mine too.

This is not philosophy—
But a bitter truth.
I have tested
Friendship, family, and love.

When I couldn't even belong to myself,
How could I have held expectations
From anyone else?

Life treats me like a stranger,
Yet for others,
It remains a garden in full bloom.

It feels as if there's nothing left to live for—
An entire lifetime
Lost in the mistakes of youth.

False accusations,
Heavy burdens—
Life is beginning to feel suffocating.

If not for the silent watch
My mother keeps at home,
I would have surrendered
To the agony of death—
Defeating myself, moment by moment.

I don't know why
My own grief doesn't comfort me,
Yet the sorrows of others feel familiar.

I can no longer meet
My own eyes in the mirror,
And I tremble at the thought
Of standing before God.

The stains of youth never fade,
Nor can they be forgotten.
This thought haunts me endlessly.

I keep hoping that happiness will find me someday,
That God will be merciful,
And that the one I love
Will love me back.

I don't know which fresh wound
Is waiting to bleed.
I struggle to find the words
To express my pain—
For those who once shared my sorrow
Are no longer there.

Some relationships have become distant,
Some remain upset with me.
But at least now,
Love is no longer questioned.

I have already destroyed myself
With my own hands.

I am the criminal,
The punishment,
And my own worst enemy.

I don't know what hopes
Life still holds for me.

People call happiness their destiny—
But my destination is different.
My story is not like the others.

Time demands patience,
Yet my soul is still young,
Unaware of what more suffering awaits.

But perhaps,
This is how it was meant to be.

Life was never meant to be easy,
Nor was living it.

In this long journey
Of just a few fleeting days,
A few more moments of pain and trials—
So be it.

When the weight of sins
Begins to bow my shoulders,
I remember God.

When the desires of the world
Shake my conscience,
I remember God.

When my feet tremble
On the wrong paths,
I remember God.

Knowing well that my words
Will pierce through hearts,
I remember God.

Yes, I am content—to some extent—
That at least I still remember God.
That I have not become heedless of Him.
That somewhere, somehow,
Faith still holds firm within me.

That I have not turned away from repentance.
That I have not strayed from God's path.

Neither peace nor solace,
Nor a breath of relief remains.

The mosques are no longer
As full as they once were.

Neither is there a modest veil
Over foreheads and eyes,
Nor do tongues now
Chant the praises of God.

Neither faces
Nor hearts are pure here.
Even humanity has been
Buried—by humans themselves.

Which stories should I unveil,
And which should I conceal?
Should I give preference
To my own desires,
Or should I also
Keep the afterlife in mind?

Should I be a believer in one moment,
And a hypocrite the next?

Why wait for the Day of Judgment—
When Man has already made himself… God?

Sometimes, the paths,
The people,
The time—
And everything in between—
Are all wrong.

But firm belief
Never lets the boat of hope sink.
Yes, it may crack and shatter,
But it never truly drowns.

If you look closely,
The courage of an ant
And a bird is admirable—
Then why do our own steps falter?

God tests His servants,
But if you make Him your only refuge,
Even in pain,
You will find nothing but love.

Yes—
The veil over your eyes
And the illusions in your heart
Will shatter.

Then,
You will lose interest in the world itself.
And in the solitude of the night,
With hands raised in prayer—
You will seek only Him.

When it feels
As if the earth is about to split apart,
The sky is on the verge of destruction,
And the lightning strikes so fiercely
That generations will remember—

Yes,
The only thing that will remain
Is God.

The One who brings light into darkness,
Who grants peace to restless hearts,
Who Molds dust into human form,
And who brings the dead back to life.

Today, I stayed in prostration for a long time,
As if I had returned home after ages.

The quarrels, the sulking,
The making up—it all continued.
Our conversations stretched
Through the night as always.

I was seeing myself as unworthy,
Yet He granted me the rank of supreme wisdom.
I kept accepting myself as a mere lamp,
Yet He made me shine like the sun.

I saw myself as a river,
Yet He expanded me like the ocean.
I considered myself a traveller,
Yet He showed me the destination
And brought me peace.

Today, I stayed in prostration for a long time,
As if I had met myself for the very first time.

Once, I was a wanderer,
Now I have drifted away from the shore.

Even if I lose,
This loss is one I gladly accept.

If God settles in my heart,
Even death seems beautiful to me.

Today, my heart has found its home—
For my faith has been
Strengthened through trials.

Once more,
Gently place your hand on my head.
My guardian angel,
Let me sleep in your lap again.

In this world full of helplessness,
Lend me your shoulder once more.

Even if just for the first and last time,
Hold me close again.
Let me cry—
Complaining and grieving.

Wasn't I your little child?

I don't know when,
I too became prey to this world.

In just a moment,
I grew older
Than my actual age.

And every time
When the sky thundered,
I raised my hands in prayer,
And only remembered you.

I know the truth,
And the reality of it—

Once again,
I prayed to God
For your return.

I keep track of everyone's well-being,
I try to keep everyone happy.

Even when someone drifts away,
Blaming me for their own mistakes,
I still find ways
To bring them back with love.

I worry about the sorrows of the whole world,
Yet my own state is such
That I have started
Drifting away from myself.

In the silence of chaos,
I hear even those voices
That have never crossed anyone's mind.

I have woven every word
Into a story—
As if I am the cure
For everyone's pain.

But whenever the cure fails,
I turn into a prayer.

I don't know
What kind of wind is blowing,
But with whomever my eyes meet,
A strange fate unfolds.

Feel it, acknowledge it—
At least let some regret
Touch your eyes.

Just once,
Have some mercy
On this heart of mine.

Leave behind your scent,
Your memories, your words—
Pass by me,
But stop for a moment,
Sit beside me.

I am neither your destiny
Nor your fate,
But at least show me
Some kindness.

In this world of words and thoughts,
If nothing else—
At least feel something for me.

For just a moment,
Make my story complete.

I have poured over you
Like rain in an untimely storm.
Yes, I have caused some ruin—
But it wasn't as if
Your gaze never reached the sky.

Somewhere, somehow,
You knew—
That what existed between us
Wasn't just an illusion.

But what remains now
Is mere dust,
While you were
The perfect moon in my sky,
The colour that stained
My empty palms.

Fine—
I have left you to yourself,
To your fate.

But don't you feel
Any regret
At my departure?

I thought I would pour over you
Like raindrops,
And you would find peace
In my presence.

I know you are upset—
Hurt by my sudden departure,
And by the time I took
To turn my confession
Into acceptance.

The more
I get away from you,
The closer
I find myself
By you.

I had just started facing myself,
Because I had begun meeting you every day.
There was a restlessness growing within me—
Did you start feeling it too?

I was weary
Even after the passing breezes,
But after meeting you,
I began meeting myself.

Was it really so easy for you to forget me?
Or were you just trying to convince yourself
That nothing existed between us?
But did nothing truly exist?

Yes, I know my sudden return,
My decision to finally lay my heart bare,
Has raised many questions in your mind.

Why did I take so long?
Because I was afraid of losing you.
All my life,
Whatever I desired—whoever I wanted—
Was always taken away from me.

And you—
You are the most beautiful longing of my heart.

So, watching you from afar felt safer.
But the fear of losing you still haunts my heart.

Whenever your heart seeks a shoulder,
Whether you accept me or reject me,
I will always be here for you.
With every piece of my heart, I will claim you.

This is beyond love and affection—
This is madness,
This is devotion.

In love, even separation is accepted.
If the beloved chooses someone else,
Then removing them
From the heart is an impossible denial.

In love,
A single glance is enough for a lifetime.
In love,
There is no regret, no refusal—
Only love itself must exist.

Yes, it's all about—
Falling in love,
Experiencing the love.

And I—
I accomplished the mission of life.
I explored love.
I fell for the love.

Yes—
It's all about
Love

From the beginning
To the end.

I hide you within my eyes,
Yet every day,
I long for you even more.

There are no limits left to cross,
Yet your love
Feels shallow compared to my depth.

The blush on my cheeks,
My shyness,
My lowered gaze,
The racing of my heart—
All bear witness to you.

How can I keep you hidden any longer?
You have begun to reflect in me.

I will be found
In the thorns of a flower,
And in the wounds of the past.

Sometimes in the breeze,
Sometimes in the fragrance.

Whenever you call for love,
You will find me there.

But now, I leave it to you—
You may let me turn to dust,
Or stain my purity with crimson.

You may call me
The guardian of the moon,
Or the depth of the ocean—
The center of my love.

Love me and test my devotion,
Or love me and embrace it fully.

Just let my love be yours,
And let your love be mine.

Since you left,
My heart burns out of love—
Longing,
Waiting,
Staying.

Ask my heart
How I was in love—
Deeply,
Completely,
Madly.

How do you stay so far from me,
Even while being so close?

I had heard that love is blind,
But your love fills me with pride.
It compels me
To ask for you from the Divine.

I was nothing but love itself,
And now,
I am nothing but yours.

A veil over my eyes,
A seal upon my heart—
Since you,
My gaze has not met another's,
Nor has another's love passed through me.

I say it openly,
In scattered words—
I am yours,
And you are mine.

If prayers hold such power,
Then why don't you
Ask for me from the Divine?

Why don't you claim me as your own
In this vast ocean of love?

I have never wished for anything in life,
Except for you.
Never asked for anyone but you.

How can I let another's hand
Become the moon of my palm?

Not even for a moment
Can I separate myself from you—
How then
Can I imagine
A lifetime's journey?

With someone other than you?

Everything was a lie—
The dreams, the life,
The desire of wanting,
The intimacy, and overall—
You.

And if something was true,
It was betrayal,
Perfidy,
And overall,
Your love for me.

I will turn to dust
And stand before you.
Mold me as you wish.

I will turn white
And stand before you.
Colour me as you desire.

Sometimes as the moon,
Sometimes as the face of the ocean—
See me however you choose.

I will be found
In the thorns of a flower,
And in the wounds of the past.

Sometimes in the breeze,
Sometimes in the fragrance.

Whenever you call for love,
You will find me there.

But now, I leave it to you—
You may let me turn to dust,
Or stain my purity with crimson.

You may call me the guardian of the moon,
Or the depth of the ocean—
The center of my love.

Love me and test my devotion,
Or love me and embrace it fully.

Just let my love be yours,
And let your love be mine.

Who knows what I must have endured,
How lonely the nights must have been.
Time refuses to pass,
Without you,
I am no longer myself.

What kind of love is this,
That I have only received in fragments?
What kind of beloved is mine,
Who came to me after so long?

I used to tell,
"Keep writing me letters,
And send your picture along too."

Far from you,
Far from our meetings,
I lived in constant fear—

What if you
Turn me into just another tale in your story?
What if you
See me as nothing more than a withered rose
From an old book of yours?

Deprived of your love,
I remained a stranger to myself.
Ask me—
How have I lived without you?

Every day, I plead with life,
"Be kind to me, just once.
Turn into love, just once."

And when a miracle finally appears,
I feel afraid—
What if these joys, wrapped so beautifully,
Hold yet another painful story within?

What if, upon the wounds that are healing,
A fresh scar is carved once again?

I say that love is one—
It is God,
It is paradise,
And then it is philosophy.

This is the market
In the name of city—
Here, hearts are sold
In the name of love.

I fear eyes—
Eyes that capture mine.

I fear people—
People with hidden masks.

I fear connections—
Connections that emotionally attach.

Let all your past
And hard times be mine
Take all my happiness
And fate as yours
I want to complete you with my incompleteness,
Conferring the love
You truly deserve.

Till when can a person
Live with lies?

Till when can a person
Love a liar?

To love someone
Is to love yourself.

And to love yourself
Is to love Almighty God.

You have crossed miles,
And you have miles to cross.

The sky that you see—
Is where you have to be.

Be love,
Kindness, joy, peace, and happiness.

Be all the colours of your sky.

Before you *be* for someone—
Be for yourself first.

We express love—
With and by what
We experience in love.

We define love—
With and by what
We are given in love.

Love is in the consistency—
How God loves you unconditionally,
Knowing the very fact—
That you have disobeyed, displeased,
And destroyed yourself
In the worst ways you possibly could.
Yet, His love remains rooted.

He provides your necessities,
Shelters you,
Bestows upon you abundance—
Blessings and favours,
Time and time again.

Even when you fall into sins
Knowingly, intentionally,
Still, His love is constant.
God still loves you—
More than any bond you have
With people or even yourself.

His love is divine,
Supreme of all.

How come you don't fall in love with Him?

From birth
To death itself,
He has only loved you.
He has only forgiven you
In all the ways.

His love—
It should be the first
And the eternal,
When the word *love*
Splashes through your mind.

The only love I call out,
All loud—
It is *Everlasting Love.*

A love that stays grounded,
Lasting,
Deep-rooted.
Always.

When dark, heavy clouds rush towards me,
I remember you.
When people's interest in me ends,
And they leave, I remember you.

Sometimes, even the moon appears
As lonely as I feel—
As if it too, remembers you.

When I hear the word *"love"*
Or tales of romance,
I remember you.

When I hear about the miracles of prayers,
Or the examples of God's power,
I remember you.

Sometimes, I let go of the present to fate,
Wondering if patience, waiting, or prayer
Might please God enough
To write your name next to mine.

When I feel suffocated within four walls,
I remember you.
When I want to sleep for a moment,
But thoughts keep me awake,
I remember you.

Sometimes, when I want to call out to myself,
Or when I fear losing myself,
I remember you.

When I get lost in the crowd of the world
And struggle to find myself,
I remember you.

When I start to think about life,
I remember you.
When I seek happiness,
I remember you.

When I want to make someone my own,
I remember you.
When I crave water to quench my thirst,
And peace comes along,
I remember you.

Sometimes, when I lose to myself—
When I die a little inside—
I remember you,
And in such a way
That you give me life again,
And bring me back to life.

I promise to bring you peace
Over problems that you bring.
I promise your well-being
Over time when life hits you back.

But would you promise to love me
Over life that gives closures?
When nothing makes sense either,
And I lack self-existence—
Will you become a sky that shields,
And shower love in all the ways?

Let's do it all together:
When you become fire,
I'll be cold ice—and vice versa.
When you become louder,
I'll be silent—and vice versa.

There is no
In-between
In love
Either it be
Or it doesn't

Do shattered windows
And fragile homes leave anything behind?
With the noise of silence
And dark circles under weary eyes,
Does anyone truly sleep?

Thoughts turn into dreams,
Then fingers guide them to blank pages with a pen—
But in this process,
Does the heart ever find peace?

One day, amidst a debate between
Strangers, friends, and loved ones,
I was both the rose and the thorn.

I wandered across the world,
Yet never found a home within any house—
Not even within myself.

It's true that life goes on
Even without those whose absence
Feels like life itself has left.
But after losing everything,
Is anything ever left for oneself?

If the destination
Of love is death—
Then I accept it.

If love brings ruin—
Then I accept it.

If every ending
Of love leads to you—
Then I accept it.

Love is when the person
Becomes your mirror—
Who mimics back at you.
It laughs, cries, screams,
Happy, cheerful, and silent—
Becomes your exact portrait.

But beyond love
Is when the person
Becomes your half self.

You become happy,
It makes you even happier.
You become sad,
It accompanies and solaces you in low times.

You become negative and lost,
It turns it into positive
And guides you to the pathway.

Like the half moon
At the palm individually,
And it becomes one full moon.

It's always about being through and through.
It's always about being chosen over and over.
It's when the person reciprocates love—
Rather than just exchanging
The same energy you give.

This isn't a book—
But a piece of my heart.
It talks about love,
You and I,
And life in-between.

The way my eyes search for you,
Perhaps you, too, call out to me.
Yet, I cannot see you,
And your voice cannot reach me.

It is not just a matter of time,
For this is not a wound that can heal,
Nor a wait that will ever end.

The dark evening and distant stars seek you,
Yet the radiant morning dew fails to reach you.
Dust returns to dust,
Then why this turmoil just to see you?

Why is there no honour
In a single glimpse of you?
Why does my reflection
Long in vain for your love?

All I know is love—
For love that lasts,
Of the warmth it brings.

All I know is you—
Made of love, made to love,
Just full of love.

All I know is love, you and I—
For love always lasts,
Of the peace it brings.

We are the travellers of life,
Finding the pathway to love.

And this is all I know
About love, you, and I—
It's always about falling in love once,
And rising in love all over again.

For love that always lasts,
For love that ever lasts.

I'm apologetic for the time
I've never been there—
As a kind human,
Parent, sibling, friend, or even a stranger.
Through all the ups and downs,
I've never been there.

I'm apologetic for everything you've been through,
For being treated ill, inhumanely, or hell.
Through all the ways,
I've never been out there.

I can't undo the past,
Nor can I make people
Apologize to you for their behaviour and doings.
I'm apologetic for the world
That doesn't value your existence,
Nor honours you with even an atom of respect.

Through all the pain, misery, agony, harm, and hurt—
For this sophisticated society
With its terms and conditions,
Its do's and don'ts—
Through all the lowest,
I've never been out there.

I don't lie when I say I can feel you—
Because I do, genuinely.

For the heart that has been burning,
Aching, and steeped in woe—

I know apologizing won't fix problems,
Heal hearts, or erase scars—
But honestly,
I have nothing else to serve
In your plate of life.

For it's the journey of an individual—
And through my breaking times,
Nobody was out there.

But somewhere,
I want to be the one
I always wanted in my life.

For the life that hasn't recognized your worth,
I want you to break all the stereotypes—
But this time,
I want you to do it all for yourself.

Through all times,
I want to stand with you,
Be there for you.

But through all the times,
I want you to stay strong,
Be positive.

You are the main character of your story—
Write it, re-write it, direct it.

After all,
You are the only one to have the authority
To change it, script it, and produce it.

Through and through the battles you fought,
All the dreadful compensation you bought.

Make it loud, live every day.
Through and through,
Be for yourself in all the way.

Before you wish upon people
Who could have been out there—
Be your cheerleader, your companion,
And the one
Who'd never run out of time,
Efforts, and love.

Don't pay attention to the world
That doesn't recognize your worth and existence.
Live it to the fullest—
Because this is one-time life.

Be your friend, love life,
And be the one
Who'd never ever run out
To be through with you.

One day, I could proudly say—
I'm not apologetic
For being unavailable for you.

But when you find your back,
We together scream with joys—
We are not apologetic
For a miserable life,
While making an effort to change it.

Sometimes by simply being there,
Through and through,
Over and over.

I would lie a hundred times,
I would deny a million times.
I will not let the world notice
What's inside my heart
And deep inside my eyes.

And that's how
I loved you.
And that's how
I discovered love that lasts.

Even if it can't be yours,
But completely be your concede.
Even if it isn't destined,
But can be your imaginative destiny.

I forgot how I used to look.
I don't know what it takes to
Smile, cry, and laugh—
And probably,
To be happy.

If one is not safe
Even at home,
Where should they go?

Protect your eyes
From the gaze of others,
For now,
I have begun to appear in them.

I have started meeting—
My own gaze,
Ever since I began meeting—
You every day.

What is this restlessness stirring within me?
Have you started feeling me too?

I used to be indifferent—
Even to the passing wind,
But ever since I met you,
I have begun to meet myself.

O Master of the heavens and the earth,
Today, bring my patience to an end.
O my Lord, the One who sees and hears all,
Today, grant my prayer.

Are You not unaware of my sorrow?
Then why does not my heart find peace?
If this is a test, then test me—
But at the end of this trial,
Give me what my heart desires.

Prayers made with true intensity
Can shake even the heavens.
Should I believe this is just a delay in time,
Or am I standing at the doorstep of my destiny?

You say, "Ask, for I love to give.
Call upon Me, for I love to listen."
Should I take a sign from this untimely rain?
Yet I wonder why it does not drench me.

Am I empty from within,
Or is there nothing left inside me anymore?

O Lord, hear my prayer—
Grant me that one thing,
The one thing powerful enough to change fate,
A miracle that needs no cause.

Make that one prayer mine—
Just write that one person into my life.

My eyes met mine,
In the mirror,
And the only thing they questioned—
Do I really deserve this?

How is it possible
That people do not see
The loneliness in my eyes?

This time,
I want us to meet all over again,
probably the first time,
While you fell harder
for me than
back in times
I did.

This time,
I wish for the courageous love,
And strength in my love over my fate,
To cross beyond what's already written.

This time,
I want perfect timing and plots,
For the destiny itself to plead,
To complete our incomplete story,
With a beautiful happy ending,
Where love is always chosen, cherished—
And a love that would create history
And pass to the future beings.

This time,
I want you to have all the feelings for me,
And your heart to ache, weep in silence—
The only thing that could comfort you be
My love and existence—
And my ignorance, taken for granted, absence—
Fragile you in all the possible ways,
For this is not a curse,
But a reminder of the love I sought in you
And you never willed to reciprocate, appreciate—

This is love,
Pure and eternal,
It does not seek any validations,
It happens all of a sudden,
And through all the countless falls,
It calls out the first sight of love.

This time,
I will meet you and make you mine,
When I met you back in time, I said serendipity,
I strongly believe our meeting wasn't coincidental,
But a tragic beautiful story written
And sealed with love.

Prose

The urge to change the world comes at a time when you are struggling to change your own self. You want to calm the storms of the world, yet you're constantly fighting back the war within. You aim to become who you're meant to be, to stand tall, and to shine despite the darkness. And in that very darkness of life, you deal with a whirlwind of thoughts, but somehow, you gather the courage to stand firmly against the tangible world. You find it difficult to understand your own life, but even in that confusion, you never underestimate the quiet, relentless power of love—love that brings light into the deepest negativity, that sparks hope in broken spaces, and that holds the power to transform everything.

It's all about me in the end. All the things that I deserve, all the things that I desire, all the things that I demand. For so long, I've searched for love in places that only offered leftovers, clinging desperately to anything that felt like warmth. But the truth is—it is essential to love myself first. Not in fragments, not in moments, but completely. It's necessary to step back, to give time and space for understanding—not just others, but myself. Healing doesn't come from chasing what's missing; it comes from embracing what already exists within.

I don't know what went wrong or when it all shifted, but somewhere along the way, life made me so quiet. Not peaceful—just silent. I no longer have the desire to live the way I once did, nor do I even remember what used to make me happy. Everything feels distant, as if joy belonged to another version of me, one I can't seem to reach anymore. And the scariest part isn't the sadness itself—it's the numbness that's settled in its place.

Why do you need someone to tell you that you're appreciable and capable? Why isn't it enough to pat yourself on the back, to recognize your own strength and progress? Doesn't it validate you when you show up for yourself, even in silence? You should never rely on someone else's affirmation to believe in who you are. Be your own constant. Walk your path with your head held high, not because someone else told you to, but because you know you deserve to. Life is always a solo journey—people come and go, some stay briefly, some leave quietly. But you? You're the only one who's always been there. And that's enough. You are your truest, strongest supporter. You need you—not the people, not the world. Just you.

Love is when you understand that this life is temporary, delusional, and purely experimental—a journey where you're constantly being tested through separation, grief, and loss. And yet, even in the midst of that pain, you choose to rely completely on your Lord. You hold onto unshattered faith, trusting that if this trial is from God, then you surrender, because He is the one who has written your story, and He is the best of planners. Maybe not in the way you imagined, but in a way that ultimately benefits you. Love is found in that blindness—an unseen thread that connects your heart to His wisdom. Love is in the acceptance, in the stillness of surrender, in believing that whatever He has chosen, is already enough.

Love is to feel, love is to understand, and above all, love is simply to love. It's not always grand or loud—sometimes it's quiet, steady, and deeply rooted. But more than anything, love makes you who you are. It shapes your soul, softens your edges, and teaches you what truly matters. Because love, no matter how fleeting or enduring, is worth having. It's easy to unlove someone, to walk away and pretend it never existed. But what's truly difficult is finding someone beyond love—someone who becomes a part of your existence, not just your emotions. And harder still is living in the harsh reality where you're tested by the very things you love. Where life asks you to let go, to wait, to hurt—but still, to love.

And finally, I spoke. The truth—raw, unfiltered. What I wanted, how I felt, everything I had buried under silence. Because at the end of it all, what truly mattered was self-satisfaction. Not pleasing the world, not fitting into someone else's version of right—but listening to my own heart. What I wanted, what I was willing to fight for, what I was dreaming of. A home I was building not with bricks, but with belief. A hope I was clinging to in the quietest moments. A love I was in love with—not just in words, but in every part of my being.

It wasn't easy to utter, but I did—without feeling insecure, without carrying guilt. Because I had endured as much as I possibly could. I had learned that sometimes, it's more healing to keep the wound open than to pretend it isn't there. I knew that pain and patience had no boundaries, and that it was better to release it than to bear it in silence. After all those breakout moments, after all the quiet collapses and invisible battles, the path ahead became crystal clear. It was me I had been searching for all along. It was me I was meant to return to. And in the end, the only thing that truly mattered was my self-satisfaction—my peace, my truth, my becoming.

Isn't it beautiful how you find love—and how, in its own quiet way, love finds you? I believe it's a process stitched together with patience, understanding, faith, trust, fate, and waiting. Sometimes, love doesn't come wrapped in what we desired. Sometimes, it's about how long we're willing to hold on—to a person, a dream, a feeling, a life—not to possess it, but to believe in it. To know in your heart that it's yours, even if it was never written in your fate.

And when the time comes to let go, you don't lose it. You carry it. You become content that you met them. You become grateful for the time you shared, for the way they made you feel, for the version of yourself that bloomed in their presence. You become thankful that, with all the maturity you could gather, you chose to part ways while keeping them alive within you.

Their absence might hollow you out, piece by piece. And yet, you live. Not by moving on—but by carrying them forward, silently, endlessly. And that's okay. We are human. You are not alone in this kind of survival. We've all felt it. We've all stood on the edge of heartbreak and chosen to keep breathing, even when it hurt to exist.

This is how we're shaped—from solitude, from sorrow, from shattering. Like glass of hearts designed to crack and break under the weight of love and promises. We grew up hearing that time heals all wounds, but no one told us that sometimes, Time can't compensate the damages about in the first place. And leave us regretful throughout the lifetime.

It is true—we fall in love, we fall for love, we love to be loved, and above all, we live for love just to love. Isn't love enough? And yet, it's the one thing we urge for, the one thing we're in desperate need of. In love, nothing feels wrong. Even the wrong begins to feel right. But somewhere along the way, do we not begin to overrule ourselves for love? To lose the parts we once protected. Why does it be so? Why does love drive us to madness? Why does it consume us to the point where we become sick of the very thing we once craved?

Thousands of questions rise—endlessly, restlessly—questioning love. And yet, somehow, the answer to all of them is simply… love.

When it all takes is courage. Not the absence of fear, but the quiet strength to rise—again and again—no matter how many times you've fallen. What truly matters is not the fall, but the way you strive and thrive to reach where your heart wants to be, to receive what your soul aches for. We carry hope like a second skin, hoping not for worldly gain, but for the healing of the void within us—for desires that live deep in silent corners of our being. We all long to be seen, to be known, to be valued—and above all, to be loved.

We are not cowards. But we do fear. We fear outcomes, we fear indifference, we fear being forgotten. And still, the courageous soul chooses to take the risk—knowing that whatever tomorrow brings is already written, but never mistaking fate for delusion. Courage doesn't sell you false hope; it offers clarity. It sharpens your path, it steadies your feet, it teaches you to move forward—not away from pain, but toward purpose.

And maybe, just maybe, courage is how you finally find where your heart truly belongs. Where the peace of your soul seeks has always been waiting for. Yes—it's courage that turns the table.

If life gives you even one moment to live—truly live—then be happy. Don't wait for people to validate your worth or make you feel seen. It begins with you, it exists within you, and in the end, it will always return to you. The moment you're in right now? It will fade. It will pass. And you don't want to look back with regret for not embracing it when it was yours. If this is what you need to hear—then affirm it. Say it. Manifest it. For yourself, by yourself. PERIOD.

Do you know? I feel empty these days. No—you probably don't. Because if you did, you would have taken a step toward me. You would have hugged me, consoled my heart, and tried to understand the silence I've been carrying. I was just a few steps away, not unreachable, not lost. But my beloved, I tried—every possible way, every silent plea, every hopeful moment. And now, I'm tired. Exhausted. Not just physically, but in the way that even rest doesn't heal.

My mind is overcrowded with thoughts, spiralling endlessly, while my heart feels both pathetic and hollow at the same time. I don't know how to put it into words anymore. Isn't it true that our eyes sometimes say what our lips cannot? Didn't you ever think that if you simply asked, I would have poured my heart out to you? Maybe not even for you, but for myself—because I can't keep it all in anymore.

It's becoming more difficult each day to keep myself busy, to distract myself from everything I'm feeling. But every night, it becomes harder to cope. There's a long road ahead and it feels like life is throwing trials one after another. I'm not scared of failure. I'm scared of losing myself in this process. I carry all my fears inside, hiding them behind smiles and tired eyes, pretending everything is fine.

Sometimes, I find myself happy, even grateful—realizing I'm living a version of the life I once prayed for. But in the very next moment, a wave of melancholy rushes over me. A sudden guilt settles in. How can I feel like this when I have so much? How can joy and sorrow exist in the same breath? Is it wrong to feel empty when I know I should feel whole?

Or is this just the quiet truth of being human?

I'm disturbed—scattered by life in ways I can't even explain. Sometimes, I feel like I'm living in a completely different world, one that only exists inside my head. But no, I'm not abnormal. I'm completely normal. Isn't that what a heart is supposed to do? To feel everything so deeply, to carry emotions to the edge of extinction? And no, I'm not overthinking I just exist in a scenario, one that loops over and over in my mind.

Don't blame me for the person I've become. I didn't ask for this version of myself. I'm helpless, even to myself. This is life—it's where it's taken me. I didn't become this way overnight, and I certainly didn't do it all on my own. Time had its way, and I had no choice but to follow. I have an explanation for everything—every silence, every breakdown, every unspoken word—but the real question is, would you even listen?

We may not be written or destined to be together, but I'll keep those moments, memories, joy, and happiness tucked away—hidden somewhere deep in the core of my heart. And that is love, exactly choosing to love someone at the peak of pain and breakouts. Because love is acceptance. It's accepting the reality that if someone's fate isn't written in your destiny, then no matter how much you wish for it, they won't stay. Their happiness becomes what matters most to you, and that is the purest form of love—when you abandon your own desires for their sake. Because love isn't something to be taken forcefully. Love is free will.

It must be let go if its path doesn't lead to the same destination. Let go of the love, for love itself seeks the happiness of the one it loves. Let it all go for the sake of your heart—for the heart that once cherished the beauty of falling, of love happening at all. Maybe it's not always about lasting. Maybe it's simply about falling in love and experiencing what love truly feels like.

You may think that you don't fit into this world, or some prolonged questions may trigger you—why always me? Am I not good enough? Do I deserve this? Doesn't God love me? Or maybe… does He hate me? If it's already written, then what am I supposed to do? Am I ugly? Why does it always end in melancholy? Maybe I'm a burden… but am I, really?

To all the questions left unanswered, to all the things seen yet left unseen, to all the unsaid words left unheard—yes, they weigh on you. They sink slowly into your soul. But only until you truly believe in the supreme power of the One who said to the universe, "Be," and it came into being. The One who created the planet Earth for humankind and bestowed mercy, providing everything—from carbon dioxide to livelihood. The One whose sovereignty is so absolute; He could collapse the sun and moon with a single command. The One who shaped man from clay and will raise him again after death. The One who is eternal, everlasting.

Life, when lived with God, becomes pulchritudinous. It becomes a life where you're content, where you begin to understand things more deeply, where you learn to balance everything—especially your own desires—so you don't let them mislead you. Your heart softens. You stop overthinking every moment. You stop worrying about what's next. Instead, you believe in God, and you leave every single matter in His hands.

Love? How could you ever believe that God doesn't love you? Or that you shouldn't love the One who created you? The One who made you exist when you were nothing. The One who heard your silence, saw your invisible tears, and felt the heaviness in your heart. The One who granted you what you wished for, accepted you with all your flaws, and forgave you even for the things you weren't sorry for—or couldn't forgive yourself for. The One who knows your worst sides yet still covers you in goodness, lets the world see the best of you, and honours you with respect even when no one else sees the pain you carry.

The One who has promised you tranquillity, contentment, prosperity, favourable outcomes, understanding, and an everlasting love with a never-ending life.

Don't run after big achievements just to have something grand to celebrate—cherish the small opportunities instead. Do what you love, even if that means living life on your own terms, in your own rhythm. Because in the end, it's you who shapes you into a better version of yourself. If it brings you happiness, then let that be reason enough to pursue it.

Live freely, live fully—but most importantly, live the way you love to, not the way people expect you to. Not by society's norms or under the pressure of family expectations. A colour loses its authenticity when mixed with too many others—don't let your colour fade away.

Be the colour of love, the colour of life.

Simply be yourself.

Because you make you—a beautiful you.

Love is when you understand that this life is temporary, delusional, and merely experimental—a place where you are constantly being tested through separation, grief, and loss. Yet in the midst of it all, you choose to rely completely on your Lord. You hold an unshattered faith, believing that if this trial is from God, then you surrender, because He is the one who has written every word of your story. He is the best of planners, and perhaps—whether it's this way or that—the path He has chosen for you carries a hidden benefit meant only for you. Love exists in that blindness, in that surrender. Love is in the acceptance—the quiet, unwavering trust that even when you don't understand, you still believe.

Love. How beautiful the feeling is—when people fall into it as if nothing else matters, as if there's nothing more and nothing beyond to be held. It brings you back to life. It makes you feel seen, important, like your existence finally holds meaning. Love varies with people, shaped by their experiences, by the chapters they've lived through. And yet, somewhere along the way, people begin to curse love.

But the problem isn't love—it never was. The problem is people. Love, at its core, is pure. It's sincere. It's empathetic. But people come into it with demands, with expectations that twist love into something greedy, something conditional. I find it cruel, honestly—how people change with time. How easily they unlove those they once loved so deeply. Where did all those efforts go? All those prayers? All that unspoken, burning love? Were they meaningless?

Was it recklessness? Or did hope simply to vanish once they received what they had once longed for? It's pitiful to witness—to see someone unlove, undo, and walk away like it never mattered. Was it always meant to begin just to end this way?

People change, yes. But love doesn't. And whether we believe it or not, love always holds that soft core. Always.

It was difficult to know if it was truly love, or just the illusion of it—or maybe it wasn't love at all. But after everything, you come to realize that the hardest decisions made during the worst phases of life are what eventually guide you to where you're meant to be. From heartbreaks and detours to wrong timings and painful lessons, every step sharpens your vision. It teaches you how to judge more clearly, how to consider what matters, and how to deal with things with strength you didn't know you had.

And then, you understand—it was never really about the love lost or the people who left. It was always about your self-esteem. The most important thing was choosing yourself over everything. Prioritizing your peace over pleasing others. Putting yourself first—not out of selfishness, but out of survival. Over relationships, over people, over society and the world— it was you who always mattered most.

Love can be anything until it becomes your everything. It can be running after a dream, doing whatever it takes to make it come true, in any terms of possibility, to make it worthwhile. Or it can be being career-oriented, striving to see yourself at a higher position, working tirelessly to achieve success, paying off all those late nights, working until the morning breeze, fuelled by ten cups of coffee just to stay awake, fighting with your own self to give your best.

Sometimes, love simply means understanding what you want to do, what you want from life, how you want things to unfold, and overall, what satisfies you. It's about what makes you content, what brings joy, happiness, and peace into your life.

How do I put into words what's in my head? A big bang theory of "What if this?" or "What if that?" or "What tomorrow brings?" The fact that I'm my own destruction—where did I go wrong, I wonder. If it was all universal, already written, then what am I supposed to do? Live a life full of suffering, or love, full of absence? Or life, full of serendipity? And, in the end, it's all for a reason.

I laughed so hard that tears rolled down, and I cried so much that I ended up laughing at my own existence. I realized how pitiful it is to feel happy when you're unhappy, like a wretch. It doesn't matter how broken I am, or if I have hateful speech, or if I became my own enemy. I stopped living in daydreams, stopped expecting anything. I've grown more realistic in this materialistic world, surrounded by filtered people who are ugly behind their masks.

I'm okay with duping myself, rather than letting anyone come and scatter me. It's okay to pin yourself down than to be stabbed by those you call yours, or beloved, or blood. I'm not harsh, am I? I'm just trying not to let myself lay down and let people walk over me. It's all okay to be ruthless.

Know when to cut unhealthy, abusive, or dysfunctional relationships, negative energies, bad environments, or people who bring you down. Don't beg for love, because if you do, you're allowing people to downgrade you and laugh at you. Understand that this is not the love you're looking for. If you continue to chase it, you're running toward the destruction of your own life. You are your own destructor.

I wonder how nothingness pulls you apart when you want to love someone without having them, when you want to live without truly living, when you want to be happy but can't seem to feel it anymore, when you want to cry but have no tears left to flow, when you want to die but you really don't want to. Is it too much? Or am I pathetic? Maybe I'm just emotionally drained, exhausted, or tired. I wish I could sleep for a few seconds, some minutes, a day—maybe forever. I'm lost in wonder.

You calm the storms of the world, but you're left behind in those dark nights when you want to scream but don't want anyone to hear. You want to reveal your scars but also want to keep them confidential. Am I imposing on someone? Is it intolerance to uncertainty that makes me want so many things—wanting people to know me, without truly knowing me? Is that too much? A big ask?

The four dark walls, with a beast inside. I'm afraid I'll be next. I fear not the night, but the light doesn't compensate. Because crime is a crime, and it can happen anywhere, at any time.

Things I never said: Behind a happy face, there is a frustrated side nobody knows. Behind a kind heart, there is a void full of sadism. Behind a beautiful life, there is a phase of vicissitude. And behind living boldly, there is a drawback. Will you listen to the silence? I do. I do it most often. What do you want me to spell out? What do you want me to hear? How do I tell you what's in my mind, and what I'm going through in my heart? To all these questions, I have a prolonged answer. Darling, you'd get tired of me, or maybe you'll leave me apart. Don't. Just don't. Because those are things I never told anyone. In fact, I lack the courage to talk, even with myself.

I always wanted to share every detail of how I've been. Childhood is known to be the best phase of life, where we become what we capture by watching everyone around us. But what if I told you that for me, it wasn't less than trauma, a nightmare, or maybe worse than anything I could ever expect or ask from life? I was called dumb, incapable of doing tasks properly. I was compared to my peers—my age group, with their ability, capability, and adaptability towards the curriculum, socializing, and engaging with the world boldly. I wasn't what they portrayed me as, but their perspectives didn't just change their behaviour toward me; they changed how everyone saw me.

I was punished every day. I was starving every day. I was bullied every day. I was abandoned. I was forgotten. It was a lack of existence—or maybe dusted in order to be unrecognizable, or maybe easier to get rid of in order to burst into agony. We are built by what raw materials we fit in. It's time-consuming, energy-consuming, requires planning, substructure, excavation, roofing, framing, and finishing. But we are built by what people fit into us—peer pressure, climate of opinion, consensus gentium. Sometimes, it's not what it seems.

How do we grow older at a young age? How does maturity take place within us? How do we part ways in life, escaping reality by running toward nowhere? How do we make things up to justify our actions—to prove people wrong or, maybe, for the satisfaction of proving it to ourselves?

I don't know if I deserve to be treated this way or if people around me are revenge-takers, or if their happiness lies in ruining someone's life, maybe mine. Now, I'm okay with everything. Whether people are with me or not. If life is taking this path, I have no complaints left. No regrets for being pitied or guilty for the things I was blamed for or how I was portrayed wrong.

Things I never said: There are always blessings hidden in those breakouts. Whatever you are going through is bringing you closer to something you never witnessed in dreams, or in reality itself. It's about failing, falling, and fighting for what you want and what you deserve. The truth is, the world captures you. This is life. I knew it too early, or maybe late, but it calmed me anyway. I know it all—the reality, the end—and I'm so thankful to myself for accepting everything that comes my way to break me, heal me, destroy me. To be honest, now I don't feel things at all. It doesn't matter to me anymore, or it doesn't require me to look forward, to check in, to take care or control of people, things, or the world.

I marked something for sure: I will never settle for less in my life, even if it costs relationships, family, friends, or people I call mine. Nothing and no one is superior to my well-being and my future, even if I have to cross all boundaries, without following the blindfolds others give me to please them, to beg them for a secure life, or to fall in love with life. After everything that has happened to me, I'm glad I've made it this far, fighting anxiety, depression, nervousness, tiredness, negative thoughts, evil powers, and self-hatred. Maybe yes, this is life—a life full of rollercoasters, lies, love, struggle, joy, and complications.

Maybe this is life, where it takes all of you in the name of 'Love.' And you live a different life. In love, you love all things, the person, even the ugliness. But when you are out of love, you despise the very things you once loved. When rain doesn't bring peace to your heart, or when you want to cry but can't, even if the tears come, they don't bring you ease; or when you feel short of breath but death doesn't part you; or when you want to sleep but nightmares won't let you; or when you want to live again, but life seems to be at an end. Or maybe when you want to give love a second chance, but all the pain that's happened to you screams in your head, begging you not to break your heart again. Or when you want to escape, but everything around you remind you of past experiences, not allowing today to become another bad patch in your life.

There's no intensity of pain because it's given by someone you loved the most. But in life, nobody owns anybody. We meet, we separate, and we grow in between. Trust me when I say that you live with or without what you love. Even if death parts you away. I lived those nights that were way easier than dying, because suicide is not an option—it's the end of everything. I knew, I knew it all: this is a 'one-time life,' every single thing, from the moment we're brought into life until the last breath, when your existence will no longer be recognized, resembled, recalled, or remembered. There's no validity to it, no assurance that might make you feel successful or valuable, where your worth in life feels like just a piece of cake.

My eyes have not slept for so long, my waitings have witnessed awaiting someone who is not meant to be mine. My nights are more like nightmares than calming clouds, my heart is more melancholic than the deadliest volcano, and my feelings are more like metaphors than poetic wording. Am I an overthinker? No! I simply think of the coming storms, calamities, or maybe thunderstorms in the face of humans, things, or life itself. I don't know why people call me an absolute human, like an alien on the planet Earth, just because I'm different from other beings. They might call me boring or too old-fashioned for kneeling to literature and being poetic all the time.

I felt that calmness in poetry where you are not misunderstood or left alone. Poetry helped me to come out of certain things, people, and times. Isn't it so beautiful how poetry captures emotions when you truly believe that words are not enough to describe what you're feeling or what you're going through? Yet, that wordplay in poetry hits you hard, making you realize how easily poetry can comprehend your feelings, like a solid candle melting deep down slowly.

How beautiful it is to elaborate, exaggerate, enhance, and emphasize everything in poetry—beautifully and easily. Isn't it? I'm mesmerized to see how powerful words are, and yet, how they eventually reveal weakness at the end.

I don't remember the last time I smiled with my whole heart and soul, but yes, I do remember when I pretended to be happy, both inside and out. I grew and learned, ages ago, that nobody cares about how you're doing in life. Yet, I assumed people were tender in nature. Well, yes, it was my fault for having the least expectations of myself and excessive expectations from people who never cared about my past or present. Its fine reality is harsh and cruel. I don't run from the fine line that even I am part of society, and I am the society that once had negative, judgmental opinions of others.

Nobody ever told me that it's okay to be wrong sometimes, and that I might overreact. But yes, it's true that none of my family, friends, schools, or even society ever taught me that "forgive and forget" are principles of life. I wish they had taught those things. I bet I wouldn't have become the beast I am today.

I feel sorry that I was born in this sophisticated century, where I am the only crime, and the only punishment is to die in agony and angst with every breath I inhale and every breath I exhale. I was not alone in this period of time or in this phase of life. And if I am wrong, then every single person is wrong—from my parenting to my schooling and society, because none of them ever taught me the thin line between right and wrong. If I were to be punished, then everyone should be punished, because everyone was an equal criminal.

I was a lost child in this big city. I searched for a lap and a shoulder to cry on, a hand to hold, and a heart to listen to, to guide me through the journey, to show me where I was going wrong, to point out my fault. But miles and miles away, I saw myself alone. I was completely forgotten, and my existence was no longer remembered. I became a dust-filled memory.

Isn't it beautiful how you become a different person in love, being in love? How it beautifies everything around you, how you become happier, and how impatient you become when you don't find yourself around the one you love? How courageous you become, willing to do anything to be with the one you love, and how it makes your life purposeful, settling your heart at peace.

But certain things shake me—how a person can become a beast coming out of love, how numb someone becomes after losing the one they love, how love transforms a wholesome person into a criminal, and how it overpowers a person, making them selflessly selfish in wanting to own the one they fell in love with. We may meet accidentally, but life has purposeful intentions to cross our paths.

How mesmerizing it is to find love and how love finds you. We love once, immensely, honestly. We fall in love again, not because we are unlucky in love, but because love can be felt again and again until we are content with it, with the person. Love can happen anytime, anywhere, with anyone—whether it's meant to be or meant to part ways. It's always beautiful to fall in love with the right person, or maybe when the right person turns out to be the wrong one, or when the wrong person becomes the worst part of your life, creeping through your past.

Don't look for perfection, because the beauty lies in imperfection.

People may find it strange, or it may amaze them, but you know the unknown truth behind it—how the world moves around you, rushing somewhere, while you are stuck. Yet, a world within you moves to rush nowhere, and you simply sit at the corner of the window, observing the world. You create a tiny universe full of peace, happiness, and joy, where there is just you—no brawl, no farce, no wrangling. And you enjoy being this way, in a way that separates you from people, where their absence doesn't make your heart numb or your eyes cry.

You become satisfied with yourself and your life, where you admit and adapt to the things that come your way or pass by your way. If it's yours, it will surely find a way to you, no matter how far you are, or if you want to let it in.

I still remember the last time I felt the happiest, or when I laughed so hard it squeezed my lungs out, or when I had the most amazing day. I remember capturing those moments forever in my heart, like a framed photo of home. I remember feeling embarrassed when I was caught having a dirty mind or being silly, or when I felt cool enough to be myself. I remember when I lived a life where I loved living, fully present in each moment.

I knew this is something we all urge for, yet we can't claim, own, or owe it. Sometimes, we just need to live in the moment, without asking more from it. Time flies once, but it reminds you again and again. Don't let the walls you've built ruin your happy times or the relationships that bring out the best in you. Live life to the fullest, because every moment you live will surely become a memory, and memories should be memorable and cherished for a lifetime.

When you mention those memories, your heart should bloom, your cheeks should blush, your voice should shiver. When the sky turns blue, purple, and white, and when time slows down, and everything around you become beautiful, where you romanticize being raised in love, then falling, because friends are meant to be forever. We always raise together, grow together, love together.

It's not about coffee, late nights, or vacations—it's about conversation, acceptance, and maybe just a few moments of togetherness. It's about being willing to make an exception, turning dreams into reality, walking hand in hand, from a street to the never-ending road of life.

I was waiting for some conversations to happen, waiting for a moment to feel understood, but instead, I broke down into millions of pieces, turning grey. The palpitation, the chest pain, the shivering body, the numb heart, teary eyes, and a blank mind. Do you still expect someone to write it, to feel it, when their life feels like it has come to an end? The sufferings, the suffocation, the mental breakdown, the physical ache, the emotional damage.

I wish someone had ever forced me to open up, then maybe I would have revealed what I carry within. Have I ever told anyone? That there's a burden on me, or that my heart feels heavy inside? Or that those touches in love felt inappropriate? No. No! It wasn't love. It was an assault, harassment, sexual abuse. If those tantrums hurt me, if they broke me inside.

Did those moments spent listening to jokes ever really matter? They did. I felt it the most. It took everything I had, all my courage, to speak. It took everything I wish I had now. How do I tell you how much I fear? The people, the walls, the norms, the voices, the night, the darkness. You'd call me an idiot if I told you that I fear the cry and bark of dogs, or maybe even my own shadow.

How do I tell you all of this when you never asked me? Please don't say that needs should be asked. I can't. I am at a phase in my life where I feel like I'm imposing on someone, or maybe I'm bothering someone. How do I tell you? How much I hate myself nowadays for the things that once made me the happiest. I know I'm no longer the person you once knew, but I can't find another way to get back to you. It's so hard to start everything over, or maybe continue from where we left off. I'm trying. I'm really trying my best.

But will you help me come out of it? Will you be gentle, soft, and kind to the broken pieces of my heart? I know it can't be fixed now, but what's broken is already beautiful. Isn't it? Don't worry about getting pricked, because the pieces of my heart don't harm or hurt anyone except myself. I hope my waiting doesn't last too long, that I'm finally held. And yet, I'm lost, communicating with myself in my head, waiting for your response to contemplate.

To all the times I kept myself unspoken, flashes in my head, making me scream out loud. To all the times I stood strong when I wanted nothing more than to break into tears. To all the times when I said I didn't feel it, but I felt it harder. To all the times when people believed what I wanted them to believe, I longed to set my soul free, just for one last time.

However, I still lack the words to express what I feel right now. It's beyond anything anyone could ever describe. Sometimes, it becomes so much worse, and I can't find the words to explain what I'm going through. To all the times I thought I wasn't enough, that I wasn't capable, that I wasn't worth it. To all the times I thought I was just a mess, just a waste, completely hopeless, completely helpless. To all the times I felt lost, like I was done.

To all the mixed feelings that overtook my courage, my strength, my conditioning, my penitence, my beliefs, my practices, and my overall deliberation for yearning to end it all.

All the things that took place were temporary and necessary. Life has to move on anyway, and so do you and I. With time, you'll thank every single thing that happened to you, for it made you stronger, brighter, and a fighter. There are always blessings hidden in the turns of life, where you're tested with what you love, what you want, and what you need through breakups, separation, and the departure of the close people with whom you once thought you'd spend your whole life. You'll realize how important it was to be tested in life, in love, to see who is truly meant to share life with you.

Trust me, bad days, worst phases, and hard times don't last forever. But when they come, they bring reclamation, satisfaction, and glad tidings for standing firm, being patient, and trusting the process of life. And it's there, in those moments, that you truly taste every relationship. The people who are yours will be yours at any cost, and the people who are not yours will never be yours, no matter how much you beg them to stay. You'll rationalize that sugar, and salt can't go hand in hand.

At first, you may feel numb to their change in behaviour, but with time, you'll realize they were with you for their own perks. Maybe you never mattered to them as much as they mattered to you. They could've respected your emotions, but they didn't. You'll adapt to how ordinary they were, and you'll realize that they mattered to you because you gave them so much importance. They could hurt you so badly that it feels like it takes a lifetime to heal but let them go as if they were never a part of your life.

The right people, however, will always stay by you, even if you beg them to leave, because you are less of yours and more of theirs. Your importance in their life matters to them so much that they would rather hurt themselves than let you be hurt in the end. The right person will fight against circumstances, people, and life just to see you in peace and to make you happy, without expecting anything in return.

It's okay to lose people, but it's hard to move on without them—especially without the ones who made you, who made you come out of your box, out of that imaginary world. The ones who made you feel that you could be someone's home, peace, and happiness. It's heartbreaking to lose them, but how beautiful it was to meet them in this life and to meet them as a person. Maybe it was all about living those moments rather than having them forever. It's about cherishing their presence, even over separation, over demise. It's about being content and grateful for making those bonds, living with those bonds, and having quality time together.

Maybe it was the end of a chapter, and now it's time to place their memories in your heart.

Time changes a lot of things—change in humans, change in lives, and change in relationships. It can never be the same experience to go through it again. As life unfolds, you will take on responsibilities and prepare yourself to face the coming challenges, where it may seem like evil wins over goodness, but it doesn't. You will learn how the scenario changes with time and through people's perspectives, because one view cannot be the only perspective.

You will also see how people's opinions can blindfold you, affecting your decision-making, where trust breaks and advantages triumph. Dealing with loss will make you understand how much more valuable it is than winning something in the first place. You will realize how small the victory was compared to the magnitude of the loss on the scale of life.

Failure brings practice, and practice brings perfection. Perfection brings achievement, and achievements bring success.

You have to accept certain things in life: you can't always be someone's favourite person, or maybe even everyone's favourite person. You may no longer be on someone's favourable list, and you can't please people to call you their life, home, or love because that's just not who you are. What's truly yours will always find its way to you, no matter the cost. You shouldn't feel guilty, pitiful, or apologetic once you experience and learn through life that it's absolutely okay to let go of what breaks you down. Let go of the allegations against you that questioned your integrity and patience, the things that were unbearable, but you held onto for far too long.

You'll begin to see the truth about people—how they are in front of you and how they portray you in front of others—and finally, you'll move on.

I'm living now. This time, I've stopped chasing certain things, seeking attention from people who meant the world to me. I'm not running from my suffering and the panic attacks that haunt me every night. The love I wanted—the love I created in my imagination—I no longer need. I don't need anyone to appreciate my achievements because I know how far I've climbed to get to where I am today. Sometimes, it's better to leave everything behind and just live, rather than endlessly thinking about it. I'm content because I'm living again, but this time, it's for myself.

This time, I've made my self-respect a priority, my happiness the goal, my values in life the achievement, and I've made it a point to find myself in everything I do. The battles you fought alone prove how strong and capable you are. Things can go wrong, and sometimes your strength becomes your weakness, but trust me, we all have to pass through these situations and storms because we are destined to face hardships. We're tested with trials after trials, breakouts, and challenges to remind us that the pain we face isn't because we deserve it, but because we deserve something greater in exchange for it.

Like the sky's colour—not necessarily blue, white, but pink, grey, and purple. All the colours, shades, and layers—we are beautiful, different, and unique in the ways we possess these qualities. The stories we hold are similar and familiar, but not the same. We are one, yet not the same.

Fighting takes a lot of courage. Some people find it difficult to face the coming challenges, and they end up taking their lives because they're tired of fighting endless battles, problems, and situations that leave them alone to face it all. I wonder: Is it really suicidal thoughts or a step taken under pressure, or is it a disease spreading vastly among human beings? But I believe that suicide is never the solution to the problems people face when they're overwhelmed by those thoughts.

Let's learn, grow, and shine together. Let's be there for
each other in every way, because we all need each other.

Who would have come to my mind if not I? It should always and always start with us, from us, and to us. Nobody in between. No more lies, insecurities, explosive reactions, or human feelings apart from me anymore. I know. I know it all—birth, infancy, childhood, puberty, adulthood, old age, death, and being forgotten. I am solitude, like hydrargyrum, knowing its accuracy when to minimize its atomic energy, splitting into protons and neutrons, only to return to its consolidated state. I know it. I know how it all works—its process, occurrence, structure, expansion, conductivity, resistivity, susceptibility, and restoration.

Don't call me a sore loser or an excuse maker. I simply avoid toxicity, venom, negativity, misery, and calamity because they only lead to suffering and breaking. Is it abnormal to be normal? Or do people simply claim that being abnormal is normal, just to go with the trend?

I'm lost in wonder. Am I the only fool who let people come and fool me? I question my identity, integrity, morality, and nobility if it's that easy to cut off certain things—or maybe people—who made me feel love, then used and discarded me. Despite giving them another chance to prove their worth and place in my life, I dumped them. They made me feel regretful for being kind and generous. They made me feel like I was imposing, like I was a burden on them.

To all the things they made me feel, I now realize I should let it go instead of giving them the power to shape my thoughts, wrecking the parts of me that are still intact. They did what they wanted to, and sometimes, it's necessary for a building to collapse rather than remain hollowed inside. It can be rebuilt with more strength, but if you let its walls crumble, it risks becoming a graveyard.

I have a deep hatred for those desires that compel a person to sell their conscience. But the true extent of my hatred isn't just about losing oneself in life—it's these customs and traditions that feel like a ridiculous joke. Or rather, I should say, that customs and traditions are nothing less than an insult to me. And even in seriousness, I never resort to trivial or vulgar conversation.

I once believed that life was like a beautiful garden, but with time, I have seen it take on unexpected colours. Although I hold no grudge against colours, I despise those that stain purity—those that tarnish the essence of white. And as for people—those who, like flashy colours, have sharp tongues, harsh attitudes, and ignorant behaviours that wound innocent hearts—I detest their very existence.

I used to think that nothing in life was more beautiful than love, that love had the power to transform people. But now I understand why hatred often overpowers love, how love turns into resentment, and how it empties the heart completely.

And despite all this, hope kept me going. But not every hope lives up to expectations. Now, it feels as if everything is coming to an end. Every person, driven by their desires, is turning their life into torment. It's not that they are ignorant or mistaken—no one is more intelligent than a human. People weigh and compare everything; they choose the wrong paths and then justify their circumstances as helplessness.

How can I accept a reality that only brings sorrow, distress, and suffering into my future? Happiness is temporary, but grief is ever-present. And tell me—if happiness does not truly bring joy, is it even happiness?

I seek the calmness of the ocean in life, the kind that gives me peace. The kind that speaks without words, that connects through silent glances. One that, no matter how many times it denies, never sows the seeds of lies. Because the truth, no matter how bitter, is meant to be embraced—not replaced by deception that leaves no second chances in life.

I admire people who, like the colour white, are pure, self-respecting, compassionate, sincere, and transparent in their love. Those who, like the moon, illuminate the world, offer companionship in solitude, bring peace to weary eyes—not necessarily happiness, but at the very least, never cause pain.

Magic

There are people whose eyes shine like stars, their presence as calming as the moon, like a tree that shelters you from the heat. They hold an empathetic heart — one that understands the weight of words, their impact and cause. A soulful soul that brings solace, a kind person who becomes your pillar, your support, helping you through shortcomings.

There is nothing more beautiful than kind words, for the real magic lies within the usage of words. The root cause of human emotions is often how those words are served. Words are powerful — they can make people fall in love, pierce a heart, encourage, destroy a life, spread hate or falsehood, or take a stand for justice. They can comfort someone in low times, speak hope, or shatter someone's peace. But the real question is — what do we choose? How do we treat people through words? Do we flourish their garden of life or extirpate it entirely?

It is always words — before actions — that hurt the most. There is no deeper agony than a few sentences spoken with aggression and hatred by someone we love. Be kind with your words. Be kind with people through your words — because most are already battling with life and the world itself. And maybe, just maybe, your words could either make them feel alive again… or become a sentence to their soul.

There's a power in deeply understanding people and recognizing the truth of life. Sometimes, you admire someone's presence so deeply that you wonder what supernatural force lies within them — why you can't detach yourself. These are the people who heal, who fix without asking for anything in return. Angels, we call them. They radiate peace and goodness, showing us the parts of ourselves we cannot see. Their aura brings with it the feeling of being known, heard, and seen. When they're near, the rest of the world fades, and you — only you — feel like the one in focus, even in a crowd of millions.

When life wants to bless you, it sends fragile people. People who are caught between light and darkness. And maybe — just maybe — you are the light that can guide them out of the dark. A few gentle words like *"Hey, I'm here for you," "This shall pass,"* or *"You will be okay"* can save an entire world that lives inside a person. Be the reason people believe in goodness. Be someone others look to as inspiration.

Sometimes, our happiness truly lies in making others happy. Life isn't as complicated as we make it — we just get caught in our own spinning thoughts. We forget that *simple* is often more elegant than dressing life up in unnecessary layers. The more we simplify, the easier life becomes to handle.

Words reflect our innermost self — they show how beautiful or ugly we truly are in expression. Trust me when I say: magic is in the words — words chosen with care. Because we are human — made of emotions, of memories that don't forget, and hearts that feel far beyond what logic can define.

The Moon

To the Selene 'moon' of my life.

I have always believed that sometimes hope, dreams, and prayers take the form of a person. That one person who brings the happiness of the world to your table, the one who turns every wish you made into reality. Suddenly, every bit of life starts making sense, and you love living every single moment. Love is when it stays with you, especially during your lowest phases, like the moon. Its presence, louder than words, speaks to you. No matter how many times it may seem to deny, it never sows the seeds of lies. Because the truth, no matter how bitter, is meant to be embraced, not replaced by deception that leaves no second chances in life.
I admire people who, like the colour white, are pure, self-respecting, compassionate, sincere, and transparent in their love. Those who, like the moon, illuminate the world, offer companionship in solitude, bring peace to weary eyes—not necessarily happiness, but at the very least, never causing pain.

My beloved beautiful moon, I love you, and that won't change, even if you ask me to leave. But I will always stay, sitting beside my door, to welcome you in case you change your mind. I can't undo you and delete all of you, nor can I erase you from my mind and heart. You tell me every possible way to hate you, but I will always stand firm in my words—you're not a bad person, but time made you that way. I live that one day over again when I bumped into you on one random night, but maybe it was a special day for me, at least. How your eyes captured my attention, and your presence sealed it with love. I lived you, I loved you while daydreaming, but I was scared of waking up to a reality that tore us apart.

Through these long years, you lived within me, in my breath, heart, and soul. For the longing, I craved you, and your attention, you fictitiously loved me through literature, poetry, roses, and songs. I was never inclined to rain, but I loved it on your behalf. The times I looked up at the sky, you, 'Moon,' have always been by my side. I remember every tiny detail of how much you loved spending time with your parents, traveling, and exploring life. Gosh, I felt myself discovering how gardening made you happy, having a farm with cattle, and growing home-grown vegetables and fruits, sharing our favourite native cuisine. I remember how you flaunted saying you loved watching stars in the one-third of the night, and how your love for white colour and the aroma that calms you to fall asleep fascinated me.

I remember the days when you were as bright as the sun, where your conversation ensured that energy to vibe along. But what turned you to hide yourself behind the clouds, my beloved moon? I don't know exactly what has torn and crushed you, but I know you are intensely hurt within, and you don't want anyone to come close. The ruthless life, betrayed people, harsh reality, never-ending trauma, and life's breakouts have wiped out your heart. And now, you find relief in pain, heartache, betrayal, and you don't want to come up with a solution to fix the pieces of your heart.

My love, I don't expect you to love me, but let me love you, heal what has hurt you most, and glue all the pieces of your heart to bloom again. Because fixing you will eventually fix me and loving you will eventually let me love myself. I had so many reasons to hate myself, the way people portrayed and mocked me, but when I met you, I realized I'm here to complete you, and that eventually completes me. Regardless, I was dust, coal, seashell, and planet, and you were gold, diamond, pearl, and galaxy. I loved you without loving you, without knowing you, without touching you, without confessing to you, without confronting you. Yes, it was my mistake—a beautiful mistake—to fall in love with you. I ask nothing in return but a glimpse of you to become my saviour for life and death. I could hold onto knowing that someday someone else would love you but could never love you the way I do and can. And I couldn't hold onto knowing that someday someone else would merely love, but I fear being touched by someone I'm not inclined to.

I hated being captured in the eyes of people. If not you, nobody else is going to capture me in their eyes. My beloved moon, I loved you from afar, and I'm okay loving you from afar. I ask nothing from you—your time, attention, feelings, or probably love. Because I felt you, loved you, and that's enough and complete. It's always about falling in love, isn't it? When did it become necessary to owe it, to own it? Fair enough. I mean nothing to a person who is my everything. I lived a complete life through illusions in my imaginary world with you. From watching stars at night to cuddling in a blanket, with morning forehead kisses, a cup of coffee, helping you get ready to go to the office, while cooking your favourite meal for dinner. When you come home with a tired soul, I would hug you, nourish you with love, and absorb all of you in my arms, serving food with my hands, giving you morsels, oiling your hair, and massaging your head, reading my serene poetries I wrote for you until you fall asleep. I never asked anything in return, but I wanted to give you everything you never asked for, but deep down, you needed.

My love, you're loved by a poetess, for I'll always keep you alive in my words and in my heart forever. I accept your past, mistakes, failures, sins, and everything you did knowingly and unknowingly. I want to take all the baggage from your shoulders so you feel at ease, take all the aches so your heart finds peace, take all the problems so you have nothing to worry about, and take all the things that trouble you, giving you my happiness, fate, joys, peace, and just more love in exchange. Is it too much to ask, my beloved? You gave me one reason to hate you, but I will give you millions of reasons to love you. My love, you deserve love that lasts forever.

The real thing is, I can't undo love, nor can I unlove you, because I believe in falling into the track of love, raising and raising and raising, growing its roots deep inside the soil, flourishing its stem, leaves, petals, and flowers high above. But I don't give you the authority to walk away from my garden, smash my seeds of love, and destroy my dream garden. I loved your sincerity, simplicity, and I called you my serendipity. For the destiny that connects me with you. I don't blame you in any way for not allowing me to love you, but rather to leave you. But there are a few questions that always need an answer. If you already knew the outcome, why did you let me enter your life? If you already fell in love with someone else, then how could you have thought of me? I don't curse meeting you, but I feel pity that I met you too late. Or maybe I responded to you too late. My dreams, thoughts, prayers are full of you. Call me a psycho, but I'm enormously in love with you. And I will always love you from the depth of my heart.

My beloved moon, I'm here to acknowledge you, that I'm always here for you, waiting for you, to love you. I stand with open arms to welcome and accept you. Even if there's a zero-point one millimetre percent chance, I want to hold onto the rope of love. I can't end the storyline of our life this way and won't let you go this way. Although I never get to feel you for a while, or your presence, to lean on your shoulders, to let you become my safe place or a home I can call mine, to have long, late-night conversations until the sky turns white, to see each other through the mirror of eyes, for eyes that fall in love, understand without being acknowledged, captures those deep wounds only you knew existed, sees those unsaid thoughts you were hiding from long ago.

I wish I could hug you and feel you for once, and one last time, so it could comfort me, confine me when you won't be around, or probably when you will leave me. I want some moments of togetherness to recall and remember it all over again, to feel the essence of falling in love for the first time. It would have been enough to live a life with your memories, for love that lasts.

My beloved, Some terrible phases of life can't determine that you deserve this and punishing yourself through it doesn't mean the end of life longing for it, the pain-
This is life, we are human- full of mistakes and emotions. And things can change within the blink of an eye. I cannot see you in such agony, destroying your life through hurting yourself even more. Look around the people who love you, look within the goodness you carry. sometimes God tests through darkness- to make you learn what has afflicted you has a greater lesson in it, to learn and grow and shine through the end of life. And the darkness has its source of light. Just look around, take tiny steps towards life, live as you used to

and do things that you love to do often. İ can't undo certain things like, going backward in the past but surely, i hold onto the rope of prayers that hold miracles. And I pray one such for you. İ accept my mistake for not holding on to love tightly and now we are distant in such a way that putting things together again would probably cost a lot of damage. Because the barrier between us are certain new relations. I'm in a cupid situation because I can't let you go but accepting you will create drawbacks. Oh, my moon- don't hide yourself behind the clouds for i long to see your glance, for that's the only way of my survival. My love for you is pure and eternal. With every palpitation, throughout the end of life- I am yours. Call it love or devotion- you are mine. For the eyes that fell in love with its first glance and for the eyes that have fallen love through blindness. And yes- I call it all loud. Love lasts. Always.

-Your Selenophile-

Home, The Final Destination

Life is the beginning of the end, the hereafter, the final departure. If you haven't found the eternal love of the creator of every creation, you haven't found home. A destination with parallel dimensions and conduct beneath the universe, earth, seven heavens, hell, and the day of resurrection. Isn't life mesmerizing, to the point where it compels you to question its existence? Why life? What's the purpose? Is human life is just a delusion? What's next? Hold on, what was before? If it's creation, it possibly has no end of an end. Suspenseful and mysterious, it's something that can't be calculated through human intellect. Every system has unmatched perspicacity and conciseness, yet ceases to offer clues. Life could be a desire, a living experience, or spent in wonder. Realistically, it has its worth and value for which we will be accountable. All expenditures, assets, and liabilities will be called out to human beings, who will share the balance sheet of their lives on the day of judgment. This will be conducted vitally to contemplate how life was spent on livelihood, with a detailed report to determine and pass judgment.

The final home, the hereafter. But it doesn't end here.

Here comes the clarity of a confusion, a prolonged answer to the questions that question existence. The energy you put into worldly affairs will turn into regret. But when it is put toward good conduct, controlling desires, purifying the soul, or spreading kindness and goodness, it will be favourable. All the burdens and anguish will be shed from your shoulders, and glad tidings will be announced to those who will be granted to live forever in eternal heavens—where there is no deprivation, only happiness and good tidings for those who believed in God, the holy book, messengers, and the day of judgment.

A place neither a human can imagine nor think of its existence, but it exists for believers who, with blind faith, believe there is no god but Allah Almighty—the One. On the other hand, disbelievers who spent their lives in nothingness, desire, and who refused to accept God's existence, who lacked religious faith, and who saw life as having no purpose or value—they enjoyed worldly desires to fulfil their current affairs and needs, without ever considering that the world and life have an end. They accumulate wealth and material possessions, but they forget that truth is truth—they came with empty hands and will return with empty hands.

'The time is running, the world is turning.'

It's time to turn to reality, where there are no setbacks left in the regret of past actions ruining today's headline. It's always better to let bygones be bygones and refresh, restarting everything from the beginning. There are so many things that need to be practiced and taken into consideration so that you don't blame anyone else in the future for making the wrong decisions. It is so important to be educated and prepared beforehand. In a world where people are rushing toward a materialistic life and seeking a lavish lifestyle, they are moving further away from understanding life. How is it justifiable to be lost yet unwilling to find oneself? When you distance yourself from the purpose of life and the roots of existence, you deceive no one but yourself.

It's about finding the Almighty. It's about serving humanity. It's about being thankful for everything you have. It's about speaking for justice, and foremost, it's about taking time to give your best in every aspect of life to find your inner peace, so you can become content with giving even an atom to the world. When we completely understand the stages, phases, and reality checks of life, we live an easier life, a better life. The temporary world and short life have deceived and confused the minds of today's youth.

The Lost Generation

The lost generation. It's quite bothersome to see how every one of us is disturbed, distracted, and depressed at the same time. How we long for sadness for no reason, and nothing makes us happier either. How we've made darkness our home. It's bothersome to see how everyone is numb inside, with no purpose, no dreams, and no hobbies that excite us. The lost generation has so much to learn, to fight battles they don't talk about, to let go of what's not destined for them.

I think we've all consumed and absorbed the negativity of the world, self-hatred, and followed the footsteps of generations after generations who have lost values, tradition, and religion somewhere along the way. A generation that runs on trends that break glass, wrap it, trash it, and call it protection and awareness. A generation that is too modern to accept that people back in time were accurate at some point, where their opinions justified that they were always right, and speaking more often is what they call freedom of speech. They want to get rid of homes, families, friends, and loved ones, just to get space and privacy, to live alone as though they own nobody in the world—while, on the other hand, people are heartbroken because they're all alone in this big world with billions of people around.

The lost generation has surprisingly stunned, living two different lives—one portraying what they want to be and the other being what they aren't. A generation that hasn't lived and learned yet, but has so much to teach. The Gen Z—they named themselves because they are cool enough to take trolls as compliments. In their vivid world, they specifically have trends to follow on loop, showcasing a living standard they can't afford to maintain on their own.

The lost generation has lost its roots, questioning scriptures and religion just because they can't accept what is being commanded and offered to them, things they are obliged to do. This generation, in its vast majority, has lost themselves in this modern era, unable to shed the taboo they practice while simultaneously practicing things they don't believe in. The modern generation accepts their appearance and appreciates it but takes charge in slamming and character assassination of others. A generation that has lost its senses, chasing the wrong leaders and politicians, dividing unity and togetherness. One wrong decision can bury homes into graveyards and turn people homeless.

The lost generation hopes to find themselves again, to live with boldness and happiness, where peace is their priority, and happiness is all they want. They appreciate appreciation, compliments, and presence, despite having grudges, because they're already prepared for life. They've learned from their past experiences, and they know how difficult it is to say goodbye or how it feels to be left without a goodbye.

Love That Lasts

Love, the way to life

In life, we tend to believe that we would win at life if we perceive all the things we love. But somewhere, things that are left incomplete or left behind make us realize their value and worth. That's how the tragedy of life tests us with what we love the most. The lack of peace, happiness, and love in our livelihood is certainly because we fail to find that within ourselves, despite running to find that rope of life, hope, and love in people. Falling in love and coming out of love is a part of self and life.

We fail to understand ourselves and the state of life, which carries on the frustration and anxiety within us. While we burst on people we love with hurtful speech, we live in such a harsh world with a sophisticated society that makes us run on peer pressure, seeking validations in love, and approaching people's bizarre statements to reflect the shortcomings and doings.

Love makes our life happening, exciting, and beautiful, but we forget we have a reality check aside that makes us doubt our own self. Love is always about falling into it and experiencing the first sight of love, despite people finding happy endings. The truth is, there will always be challenges and hardships throughout life, and probably even after finding the happy ending of love stories or marriages. It might vary with people's understanding, belief system, and acknowledgment for taking relationships in the long term if they are willing to compromise their living to behold love or the one they love.

Love is the only way to live a beautiful life because love beautifies our innermost self. It makes us better humans, and after all, life is all about finding pathways through love to find our purpose in life. Love encompasses feelings, importance, and affection, rather than seeking it because love itself is a 'giver' and it never turns empty. Love has the magical power and magnetic force to transform us, to heal our wounds, and to bring light into the darkest parts of our souls. Love is not something we search for externally but something that we nurture within ourselves. It is the force that binds us to our purpose, connecting us to others and to the world. It teaches us patience, understanding, and the power of forgiveness, not just toward others, but toward ourselves as well.

Love has the magical power to change perspectives, to soften hearts, and to allow growth in the most unexpected of ways. It challenges us, pulls us to new heights, and reminds us of the beauty in simplicity. But the true essence of love is not in the pursuit of it, but in the giving of it—freely, without expectation, without boundaries. It is in the quiet moments of care, the small acts of kindness, and the deep emotional connections we form that love reveals its true strength.

When we embrace love, we find ourselves. When we give love, we become whole. Life, in its complexities, becomes meaningful only through love—love for ourselves, for others, and for the journey we're on. And in the end, the only thing that truly matters is the love we shared, the love we gave, and the love that changed us along the way.

Life, the Way to Love

In love, we tend to believe that love is the only role in life. Life has its beautiful ways of introducing you to the idea of love and the bounty of love. The treasure of the world lies in the eyes of the beholder, with the core of nurturing empathy, and in the eyes that make you visible, known, heard, valued, seen, and loved. Life has its beautiful ways of capturing you through the eyes that mimic you—like a mirror that laughs, cries, screams, beautifies, and smiles back at you.

In a corrupted world with religions and castes that draw lines between people, love is the only thing that has the power to change the world and people along with it. The world runs by people, but people run on trust, humanity, and love. And that's the magical, magnetic, and powerful way to change anything and everything in life. Love is a fixed asset of life.

We live in a state of mind where we may believe that money is the key to happiness, or being loved back by the person we love, or getting the dream job done, or taking a world tour—any number of things we want to approach. But at the very end, deep down, we yearn for peace. Peace that lies in people. Peace that cannot be purchased, but can be found in love.
What are your approaches for life? An easy life without rejections, hardships, and the worst phases? But doesn't life itself mean to learn, grow, and shine through

whatever is left in your palm? We run out of love, but it has its fixed time to come to us. Life has its own beautiful ways of guiding your pathway to love. Maybe we just need to focus on life itself in order to be prepared to receive more than we asked for.

Life has a purpose. Beyond love, we have a purpose to serve—to consider life itself as a beautiful gift and blessing.
Through and through, life will introduce you to love in different ways, parts, and things because love is the way to life, and life is the way to love.

Love that Lasts

The greatest blessing is to love and to be loved back. Love comes when you don't look out for it and leaves when you desperately need it. That's the biggest tragedy of life to make you fall harder, knee you down and weep and beg for not leaving you but despite it fragile you.

From the very beginning it was supposed to introduce you to love or maybe yourself to life. Love was meant to be happening, chaotic and energetic when it comes because it's supposed to reciprocate the love you deserve and dream especially the love you give to people, the exact same affection you needed and wanted someone to reciprocate to you. However, to love and to be loved are both special because we never know if somebody else needed that kick. Sometimes nurturing someone relieves you to the core that somewhere you don't want people to be abundant the way you were once.

If someone comes to you for any means of chance then know that you're the chosen one to help, love or to be kind to them. When God wants to answer your prayers or rip off the burden from your shoulders or to bless you with the divine abundance of happiness.

Love comes in fragments, always!. Through things, people or any means of worldly life or the spiritual journey. You are the happiest person on the planet earth to invest yourself in people or when people invest in you. The least or in abundance, if love knocks on the door of your heart then give it a warm welcome because not every single person is blessed with it. Just let it in. Even if it carries an atom weight of love. Sometimes a drop of rain has a divine purpose to becoming a wide ocean.

Most of the time we take love for granted or think that it will always be our side in all the terms we put in but when we hit the boundary it rip off the love from our heart. If love can build you then love does even have the power to turn it into dust.

Love yourself, love the people around you, love your friends and family, love your beloved one. Be kind to yourself, be kind to the people around you, be kind to the strangers you come across. Because to find happiness, peace and love is to first invest in it through and through.

Love doesn't lasts because this is the shortest life and we never know if we would to part ways, departure or maybe to catch different trains in life. Therefore, the essence of love always lasts. If you get the bare chance to love someone then do it with your complete heart. Maybe your love could revive them back to life.

Thanksgiving

Thanksgiving

I want to thank every individual reader who shared a great importance in my life in the journey of writing. Without you all I wouldn't been this best. It was you, who knew what I carry within myself when I was not aware of what it means to inspire people by just being myself with the power of writing. Thank you for believing in my potential and out comings and my debut book. I'm forever thankful, grateful of you all.

A big thank-you everyone!

Who made this book possible.

Note to Self

Darling, I want you to take a moment to listen carefully because this is really important for you to know: you're chosen by God to live this beyond beautiful life to the fullest and love life unconditionally. Here, I want to tell you that you're an amazing person because you are the best out of the best, from the old version to the bold version you're now. I know it was your courageous steps that took you on a rigid journey ahead, despite wanting to give up and letting people win over you. But you took all the necessary steps to pass all hurdles and obstacles, to test you completely and to let you break on every path. I'm proud of you, darling. I'm proud that you never settled for less, and how you fought for everything that was never easy to get. It was you who made it possible and easier. Truly, you're remarkable.

Darling, I wanted to tell you that you had all the reasons and qualities that resonate with and qualify you to be the best version of yourself. You're now imperfectly perfect for the world that has to embrace you. Your determination has always been the best part of you, showing your straightforwardness in getting things done and making things happen.

Darling, I know it wasn't easy for you to get out of bed, dress properly, have a meal, and start living again after dealing mentally, emotionally, and physically. But you did that. You've done an excellent job by not letting your dreams die. Instead, you planned, worked, and aimed. And now it's time to see yourself shining, like stars brightening and enlightening the world. Remember when you used to watch the stars from the window, hoping for glad tidings and sharing your day-to-day routine, when you were at your lowest? The stars became your hope, healing, and companionship. Now, it's your time to become that shooting star in someone's life—to make their moments magical, to grasp their sorrows, to become someone's light of hope, and to make them believe in love once again.

Some days are going to be the hardest, where every day seems harder to pass. When you look back, you might think about how you messed up everything, how you made your life tough, and you might ask for a helping hand. But nobody can save you from drowning but you, yourself. Never surrender yourself to the flow of life. Healing is important, but healing doesn't always work. It can heal your wounds, but it can never detach scars from the body. Scars never heal; people never heal, but they heal in order to come out of it. After all, we are humans, full of feelings and emotions. Isolation helps to conduct the behaviour that makes you understand yourself deeply and thoroughly.

It's always about choosing yourself over breakdowns, the end of relationships. We all get stuck in the illusions of life where we think people, society, and the world have betrayed, affected, and hurt us. But the truth is, it's us who have chosen the people in our world who made our life hell. Nevertheless, we are the only ones who have the power to change every single thing in life. We are deprived. Every single one of us is a pathfinder, but we forget that the journey begins from us, within us. You're just not able to see the love and light you carry within yourself, despite looking for it in people and their fondness towards you.

Darling, why do you forget that you're the first person who deserves your unconditional love, kindness, generosity, and empathy? When you win the war within yourself, you conquer life.

Note to Readers

My beloved readers, this journey is all yours. Without all of you, I wouldn't have made it this far. I'm pleased to share my second book after a long period of time. I hope this book helps you to understand your emotions, feelings, and life. *Love That Lasts* carries an underlined message, briefly introducing you to a long journey—one that will help you experience things you haven't felt or related to in the book, at some point in life. But once you go through it, you will understand how necessary certain things were to happen and how perfectly they were destined for you to go through them in order to find yourself.

This book is entirely, personally written for you. It is all about what you (we all) go through once in a lifetime. This book has been designed in the simplest and easiest form to help you understand. Thank you for choosing *Love That Lasts* and taking the time to read it. I hope I did justice through my wording and writing. Here, I want to dedicate this book to all of you.

Love That Lasts holds a greater message for you, one that may help you later in life. However, the book contains some religious context and beliefs that not everyone may be able to reciprocate. With due respect, it's an individual perspective, and I highly appreciate if you go through it once, or if not, then leave it as a matter of dispute.

Bidding Farewell

To my darlings, the ones who have walked beside me through every verse, this moment is bittersweet. Writing has been my refuge, my voice, my way of reaching hearts beyond my own, and through it, I found a love that lasted—a love I found in you, all. Every poem, every word I have ever written was a piece of my soul, a whisper of my heart, and you, with open arms, embraced and loved them. But now, life calls me toward a different journey, or probably a new pathway—one that does not rest between the lines of poetry but within the vast unknown of self-discovery. As much as writing has shaped me, I must now step away to truly find who I am beyond the ink and pages. This is not just a farewell to poetry, but a farewell to the writer I have been, as I seek to become something more.

Though my pen rests, my gratitude for you remains endless and heartiest. You have given me purpose, warmth, and a reason to believe in the power of words. But now, I must live beyond them. So, as I part ways with this chapter of my life, I leave you with the love we built together—one that does not fade, even in silence. Although you, all, were the only ones who believed in the potential and dreams I carry within myself.

Thank you for outshining the poet and appreciating the work I brought to the table. The author Humera Mohammed I am today truly because of you, all. I will never be short of words to thank you for the person you made me today. More than I, you all deserved this achievement and the book *Love That Lasts*.

Thank you for being my extended family and for being the most beautiful souls I've met throughout my profession.
By this, I end my writing career and journey, but I hope wherever life takes us, we're always proud of ourselves, and through love and prayers, we remain close, like the moon. I found happiness in each one of you. However, I'm the seeker of peace, finding my track of life back to where I belong through the religious and spiritual journey. I hope you all respect my decision and do not request a comeback.
'Even poets must put down their pen to listen to the whispers of their own souls. With all my heart always.

As I reach this turning point, my heart carries a weight that words can hardly hold. Every memory, every moment spent with you all, lingers in my mind like echoes of warmth and belonging. It's hard to part ways, to walk away from the comfort of your love and support—but sometimes, the journey of self-discovery calls for distance, for solitude, for change. And though my heart resists, I know this is something I must do to find myself again, in places I haven't yet explored. The love I've received from each of you is beyond anything I imagined—so pure, so healing, so complete. You have held me up in ways you'll never fully know. Through your words, your presence, and your belief in me, I felt seen, understood, and deeply loved. This journey as a writer has gifted me my greatest dream—to be valued not just for my words, but for the soul behind them. I never thought I'd be loved this way. I never thought God would answer my silent prayers so beautifully, through people like you. You've taught me that love knows no bounds, no definitions—it finds you when you need it the most. And while I may be stepping away for now, please know this: your love lives with me. It is the kind that doesn't fade. It stays. It lasts. It ever lasts.

—Humera Mohammed.

Thank you for reading.
I will be the reader of your life,
I'm just a few words away from you.

Reach me: humera6328@gmail.com
Instagram: @_humera6328

www.ingramcontent.com/pod-product-compliance
Lightning Source LLC
Chambersburg PA
CBHW031019160726
47991CB00005B/1793